Jerzy Duda-Gracz

Jerzy

Duda - Gracz

Arkady
Warsaw

Introduction: Krzysztof Teodor Toeplitz
Translation: Joanna Holzman
Graphic design: Zenon Januszewski
Editor: Aleksandra Stępakowa

Between despair and derision

When a pauper is dead, death sprinkles some food
To bait the wretch to his coffin unshod.
Mournful, his generous family resolves
To protect his bare feet from eternity's thorns.
They spend their last penny on the wretch's poor limbs
And painstakingly get him coffin bast moccasins.
Having thus dressed him up in a beggar's turn-out,
They see he's a pauper and cry their eyes out.

This is the dialectics of poverty: it is not horrifying when it is barefooted. One may even see peculiar beauty, health or simplicity in the lack of shoes, which has frequently been done in the genre or pastoral art. Clothed in a beggar's outfit in a desperate cover-up attempt, a pretentious gesture, poverty becomes openly bare and makes us weep. What Leśmian observed in his poem *Trupięgi* (Coffin Moccasins) also has a more profound meaning. The pauper's bare feet are part of nature and, like nature, have no moral significance and aesthetic connotations. They are a fact, a phenomenon, like a sunset, a leaf, water in a river. Only "shod for the coffin" does the world of human notions, by means of which people seek to control their fate by vesting it with meaning and aesthetic value, come in.

Jerzy Duda-Gracz's painting is a lament over the poverty of conventions. In the picture *Welcome, Little Daughter*, a newborn baby, with a naive smile on her face, emerges from among the nursery accessories, cushions, quilts, crawlers left on a line to dry, squeaking rubber toys and the solemn guardian angel, to plunge into the real world swarming beneath, the incredible throng of faces, figures and accessories. The confusion is only apparent as each of the elements of the inferno has a conventional meaning, the bow tie on the shirt-front of the man in the foreground, the cameo on the bare bosom of the baldish hag, the telly box, the suggestive smile on the face of the old man in a wheel-chair, the shred of a banner, the surpliced figure... The baby's life, we may surmise, will be spanned between the touching symbols of household attention and the ghastly throng of appearances of human passions disguised beneath conventional forms. The drama of this eschatology depresses us much more than the medieval or counter-reformation motif of the progress of life featuring healthy human bodies heading inevitably for the cold embrace of death. The former spoke about the *vanitas* of the mundane; the latter is stifling for the mundanity of human aspirations, that linking agent of the human condition.

Jerzy Duda-Gracz once asked a journalist: "Why do you write so much (not to my

5

dissatisfaction) about the message of my paintings and so little or almost nothing about their formal structure?" Though he contradicted himself almost in the next sentence acknowledging that he had been compared or traced back to an endless pageant of old masters (cf. reviews quoted in this book), his question was justified though it may expressed in a somewhat different way and modifed by the entries in the books of visitors to his exhibitions. Rather than asking why so much has been said and thought about the content of his works, showing through every square inch thanks to the system of lucid signs encoded in the imagination of the public, it would be fascinating to learn why the authenticity of the world depicted by Duda-Gracz has not been questioned in any of the unprofessional entries and professional reviews.

Note the phenomenon: both the public and critics write that his paintings are true to life, envigorating, painful, penetrating, hideous or ugly, that the reality on which he focuses should, or should not, be represented, but no one questions their authenticity, their identity with the world known from experience, their mimetic imitation of reality here and now. The controversy that the entries reveal is that whereas they ask whether it is proper and purposeful to tell the truth, not a single one questions the truth as such or, more precisely, the veracity of the painter's representation. It is quite extraordinary and very rare in today's art, especially the fine arts, that the public should not perceive a painter's work as one relying on his "private vision" or "inner world". In this sense, Duda-Gracz's world is not "his" but "ours", i.e., generally known and objective, and the artist presents it to us rather than creating or unearthing it and later appealing to the public for the acknowledgement of its realistic quality or tolerance of its imaginary and subjective traits. As I said, the controversy is about the conformity of representation (and its limits) to the accepted criteria of good taste or decency, something frequently discussed. Is a painter allowed to depict a nude female body? A dead body in a dissecting room? An act of copulation? The controversy is about decency rather than material truth and about painting conventions rather than bare facts.

Bearing this important consideration in mind, we now face a series of truly fascinating puzzles, related not so much to painting as to the social consciousness in which it functions.

In the history of Polish art, a deeply rooted conviction about the identity of image and objective reality confirmed by common experience was an established fact in the 19th century, as the writings of Sygietyński and Stanisław Witkiewicz indicate. But neither of the superb critics, both of whom were perfectly aware of the complexity of the painting procedure, visualised painting otherwise than as a confirmation or an analysis of what existed and conformed to the logic of experience, to the objective existence of things. For instance, writing about Maksymilian Gierymski's paintings of the January Uprising, Sygietyński argued: "Maks Gierymski gave quite an objective image of life and nature in those times; even though it does not conform to the tastes of some people or part of the public, it does conform to truth. Viewing nature and life from a painter's distance, he remembered only the general impression and later relied on it. Hence his scenes and episodes are free of the euphoria of victory or the despair of defeat, of endless fighting and decisive battles, heroic assaults and disastrous retreats; those were moments, not the general character of the movement. His paintings show detachments continually on the march, with people and horses worn out, faces more sad than happy, the whole life insecure and miserable among poor nature, grey

days, thin forests, mud, snow, cold and frost, with no food and clothing, and often with no arms either." The criterion of objective truth is even more evident in Witkiewicz when he laments over the effect of Chełmoński's career in Paris on his talent: "One who has looked at the macadam of the Parisian boulevards for a dozen-odd years finds it difficult to give a true-to-life image of the sloppy Ukrainian roads; he who has looked at omnibus coachmen and smart riders in the Boulogne Forest is not able to paint peasants forcing their way through snow-drifts, and riders cracking their whips." I have not quoted the above passages chosen quite at random to find in them, especially in the latter, a reference to Duda-Gracz's declaration: "I don't go abroad because I am afraid of losing what is dearest to me." My goal is quite different: to show to what extent the voices of the contemporary critics coincided with the opinions of the contemporary public who had seen or heard of the desperate skirmishes during the January Uprising, who had seen and known the mud splashing on the Ukrainian roads, and heard the "cracking of a riding-whip". Only by respecting this knowledge and knowing this experience could one accept a painter's work as a true representation of reality. That was exactly the way in which the public responded to painters like the Gierymskis, Matejko, Chełmoński and Juliusz Kossak.

Back to Duda-Gracz's paintings with their crowded, lumpy, bulbous reality brimming with strangest customs and conventions. As I said, it is accepted by the contemporary Polish public, frequently quite fortuitous visitors to provincial galleries, as the familiar reality confirmed by their experience gathered in the streets and homes of Katowice, Częstochowa, Warsaw and Toruń in this part of the century. That it is true to life cannot be questioned not only by contemporary painting but moreover by television and cinema, press articles, photographs and family albums, in brief, means of communication that have enforced on us an image not only different from that emerging from Duda-Gracz's paintings with an insistence incomparably greater than his but precluding the questions and associations on which his painting is based.

I am not going to play the demagogue by saying that those were "false" images created for the sake of propaganda or social instruction, and what Duda-Gracz paints is "true" because of his severe and rather grim outlook on the reality around him, and because of his perverse sense of humour. Such things may be said in the heat of account-squaring meetings, but when we are in earnest, we must be aware that societies do not like to identify with objective descriptions but with mythologies peculiar to their times. The Polish petty yeoman saw himself as a descendant of the Romans and Sarmatians and would have been mortally offended if someone had confronted him with his real counterfeit with a dirty face and straw sticking out of his knee-boots. As for the heroic period of the Polish war and the Nazi occupation depicted in contemporary literature, cinema and memoirs, who would gladly identify with a shirker, smuggler, swindler or one denouncing Jews for money? Certainly no one because the mythological image of those times has transformed us all into guerillas, insurgents, unswerving conspirators and inflexible martyrs. The problem for discussion is not whether Duda-Gracz's visions or competitive ones are true, but whether his visions, by no means flattering, have been socially accepted as apt, compatible with what we are ready to accept as our portrait.

Let us look at the paintings, their substance. What strikes us here the most is the setting, the chaotic refuse heap. The workers in the *Polish Triptych*, an ironical reference to Manet, enjoy themselves in the company of fat female revellers near a building site, with bricks scattered all

1. Lovers 2, 1968
2. Vermin (Portrait of K. Grześkowiak), 1970

over, broken planks sticking up and an abandoned concrete-mixer. The protagonist of *The High Noon* is having a nap by an unfinished fence, among waste material from the building-plot, sacks, planks, bricks, an indented bucket for mixing lime. The *Hamlet of the Fields* is shown seated among cabbage heads in the open, on a settee which is certainly not part of the landscape, but a piece of furniture thrown out to rot in the rain. Round the *Tower of Babel*, a replica of Breughel, coils of cable, pipes and knee-pieces of plumbing installations, empty varnish and paint tins, a box bearing the name of "Unitra", a well-known electric firm on it, are scattered around. Many such examples may be quoted, too many for the refuse heap to be interpreted as perverse decoration or peculiar horror vacui. Duda-Gracz's world is one of chaos and crowd, but it differs from the horrifying or enchanting chaos of Hieronymus Bosch's or Peter Breughel the Elder's canvases. They were struck by the multifariousness of the world, its unceasing activeness and obscene vitality. They were afflicted with monsters, amorphous clusters of live organisms fashioned into freaks defying logic, of the kind described by sailors who had been beyond the boiling hot waters of the equator and brought back fish and reptiles unlike those soaking in the cold waters of the Netherlands.

The chaos of Duda-Gracz's world, its monstrous refuse heap, is one of industrialisation which contributed neat, logical forms reflecting the clarity of thought and purpose of function only in the visions of its prophets and much later, at the stage of automatic sterility. Let us recall the dismay of Izabela Łęcka (the heroine of Bolesław Prus's novel *Lalka – The Doll*) at the sight of a Parisian industrial plant; let us recall Dickens, the great witness of the English industrial revolution, to realise the sense of disorder and confusion and the rancour of the world thrown off its balance by machines, steam and the chaotic movement of human masses. Francis D. Klingender's work *Kunst und die industrielle Revolution* brings, alongside images both infernal and impressive for the newly discovered technical potentialities of man, reproductions of anonymous prints of 1831 depicting a truly Boschian confusion of the industrial age. For instance, we see a violent explosion of a steam engine, as a result of which "friends of the railroad" burst into pieces, their legs, arms and heads, with an expression of doltish fear, go up in the air, and ladies, with their skirts shamelessly turned up, fall upon gentlemen lying on the ground. Or there are the draught horses made redundant by the railroad, shown as a surrealist band of street musicians playing the fiddle, bass and street organ. A poetic refuse heap of nascent industrial civilisation may also be found in the paintings of William Turner, e.g., his popular landscape of Newcastle.

Duda-Gracz has fixed his eyes on industrial refuse, the sign of our times. He sees and paints what all of us find so common that we no longer see it. Once we have seen his paintings, we casually look out of the window and become aware of the daily foray of our eyes: holes in the sloppy ground, pieces of installations, wooden packing-rooms, relics of portable fences originally meant for blocking the view of something, but in fact adding to the sadness of the debris.

Indeed, it is amazing about Duda-Gracz's paintings viewed as a faithful projection of definite reality that by all appearances something is being built all the time but nothing is built in the end. The only edifice that emerges from the chaotic bustle of the eternal building-plot is the Tower of Babel, evidently ironical and shown on a scale different from the rest, and also unfinished. Taken aback, we confront a situation different from all other visions of industrial chaos, however pessimistic, with nothing, not even an outline of a construction emerging

3. Triptych in Memory of the Artist's Father, 1970
4. Gates of Paradise, 1972
5. Polish Triptych, 1972

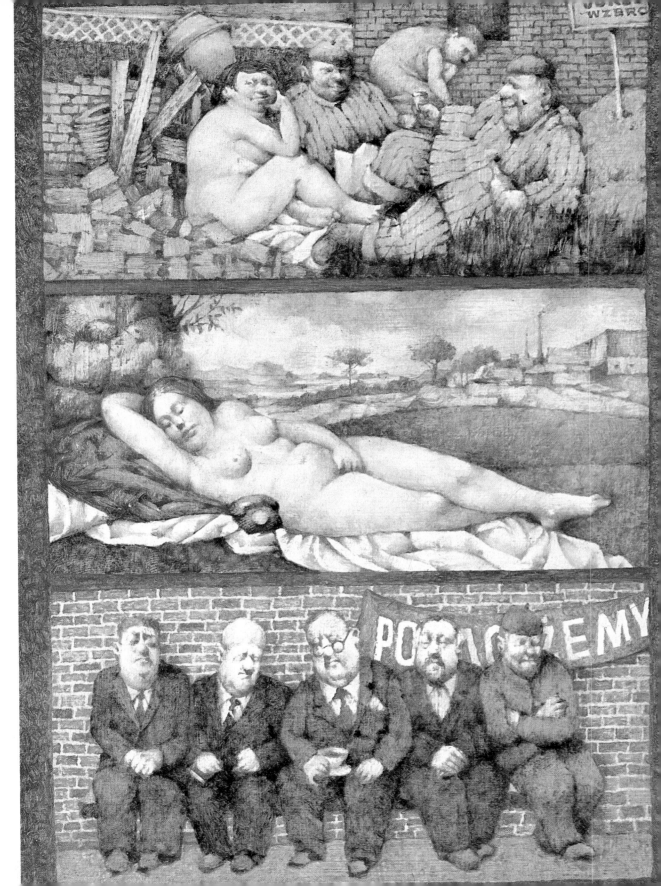

6. January Self-portrait, 1972
7. A Letter to the West, 1973

from the rubble. On the contrary, if there is something substantial and man-made in these paintings, it is strikingly antiquated. The nostalgic *Street in Gliwice*, with serene rhythm and beautifully contrasted surfaces and masses instead of the usual confusion, a work in a sense unique in our set because of its lyrical mood, shows the walls of old buildings guiding the eyes deep into a dark lane typical of 19th-century suburbs. All the pieces of the *Głuchołazy Triptych* are set against the background of dilapidated small-town architecture with an inscription in Gothic characters making us aware that a brush or a trowel have not been used here for at least forty years. Even *The Artist's Family* is seated amidst a weed-grown garden, against the background of a mouldy entrance to a crumbling house.

This is another puzzle or another paradox of Duda-Gracz's painting. The simplest interpretation of it would be in terms of the inertia that characterises most of the protagonists. Workmen, heroes of Duda-Gracz's numerous paintings, are workmen on the strength of their clothes and social condition rather than their occupation. We see them asleep, enjoying themselves, lost in somnambulic stupor or idle talk but never devoting themselves to work. Against this background, the extraordinary speed shown in the *Riders of the Apocalypse or Moonlighting*, a work so frequently discussed by the critics (NB modelled on Chełmoński's *Troika* as unreal in its run through the void of the steppe – a gallop would be out of place here) proves the rule rather than being a true exception.

I think, however, that a solution to the paradox should not be sought in the area of the evident. It is both much simpler and much more complicated. I understood the paradox for my own sake when, on my way from Cracow to the Katowice motorway, I lost myself in the thicket of semi-towns and semi-villages with which the Silesian landscape is interspersed. Goethe said that "Wer den Dichter will verstehen, muss in Dichters Lande gehen," and so I have found myself in the centre of Duda-Gracz's reality, in the world of a painter whose most profound experience originates in his native Częstochowa and Katowice where he now lives. One who drives past the small brick and wood cottages along the road where the wheels of the big lorries from the building-plots mill the thin mud, is aware that those living here work for the local building companies or the giant industrial plants. Their life is split in two. They may well build new things, but it has no effect on their immediate surroundings; what they build is elsewhere and has nothing in common with the living conditions of their families. They are manual workers, as in Duda-Gracz and, just as in his paintings, the crumbling junk round them has not been touched for years. The painter has obviously not invented this world, it is not the fruit of ingenious artistic speculation, not even a metaphor. It is simply a projection of the reality, a clever one because it draws conclusions from it.

Critics have sought to interpret Duda-Gracz's painting through the lens of its provincial pose, somewhat skittish to be frank, with decorative elements reminiscent of small town or rural markets meant to conjure up a naïve and somewhat coarse mood. Indeed, his painting provides many hints to justify the interpretation. Let us take the portrait of *The Artist's Family*, so perfectly merged with the ramshackle provincial staffage with the painter himself represented as a simpleton with a silly smile and wearing too big trousers, from beneath which his enormous bare feet are seen, and a T-shirt bearing the inscription "Poland". He is a contemporary Sancho Panza or a Candide trying to conceal a philosopher's keen eye under the guise of simple-heartedness. But the provincial key, understood as a mannersim, does not seem to exhaust the subject. It is a purely external quality which explains very little when it is not viewed against the broader background of the artistic culture of today's Poland. It goes without question that the provincial attitude or mannerism is not typical of Duda-Gracz's painting only, that it is a much broader phenomenon embracing various art disciplines. In poetry, mention is due not only to Miron Białoszewski, the eulogist of fun-fair Madnonnas, but also to Ernest Bryll and, to some extent, Stanisław Grochowiak, in whose oeuvre the provincial accessories, combined with a cult of poverty and ugliness acquired the joint name of *turpism* (term coined by the Polish poet Julian Przyboś in about 1955). In sculpture, the provincial trend with its naïve decoration, has come to the surface in Hasior and in graphic art in Andrzej Czeczot, an artist in many respects related to Duda-Gracz in his provocative provinciality. Echoes of this trend, varying in authenticity, may be heard on a much broader scale.

The variety and liveliness of the trend indicate that it is not merely a matter of mannerism or stylisation.

Their muzzles gone grey and hardened like flint
Still immersed in the shallow shrubbery of night
Snoring in their crowded carriages. Dispossessed like King John
Of patches narrower than a strip
The train proceeds through the dark. From the depth of snoring
Someone has pulled out a mouth like a fish and now drowns
Falling on his torpid alga-like hands
On the dark sand of sleep sour with sweat
This is how day comes to our town
This is the bitter tide that should shatter
Our too rosy, poorly constructed dreams
Tell me how we are to defend ourselves
When the people wake up and get off the train
and ask us "How long?" and "What for?"

I suggest we look more closely at Bryll's *Peasant Sonnet* I have quoted. Not only its stylistic tone but the underlying moral problems are also reminiscent of Duda-Gracz. The heroes of the *Sonnet* are peasants depicted in a similarly ruthless way, not far removed from caricature. Their muzzles are grey and "hardened like flint". A sleeping man has a fish-like "muzzle" and the smell of "sour sweat" hangs in the air. The royal name of King John is mentioned ironically, just as Hamlet, motifs from Manet, Brueghel or Chełmoński crop up in Duda-Gracz. It is not a brutal genre scene in provincial settings but an image of social conditions. "This is how day comes to our town", the poet says, "the bitter tide that should shatter our too rosy dreams." What are we dreaming about? Probably that we have crossed the border of modern civilisation or, more probably, that civilisation develops by the harmonious effort of society, as a result of deliberate choice and consistent, coordinated action. But the truth is quite different. Duda-Gracz's heroes arrive in our cities on "crowded trains", their sleep has broken but they are not really awake, and they use their "torpid, alga-like hands" to botch up wonders of the industrial age far away from their "patches of land narrower than a strap". Their effort is so abstract and alien to them that once they have woken up they will only be able helplessly to ask "why?" This, in my opinion, is the interpretation of the "provincial trend" in art, inspired by reflection on the ongoing Polish industrial revolution which has come upon the soporific

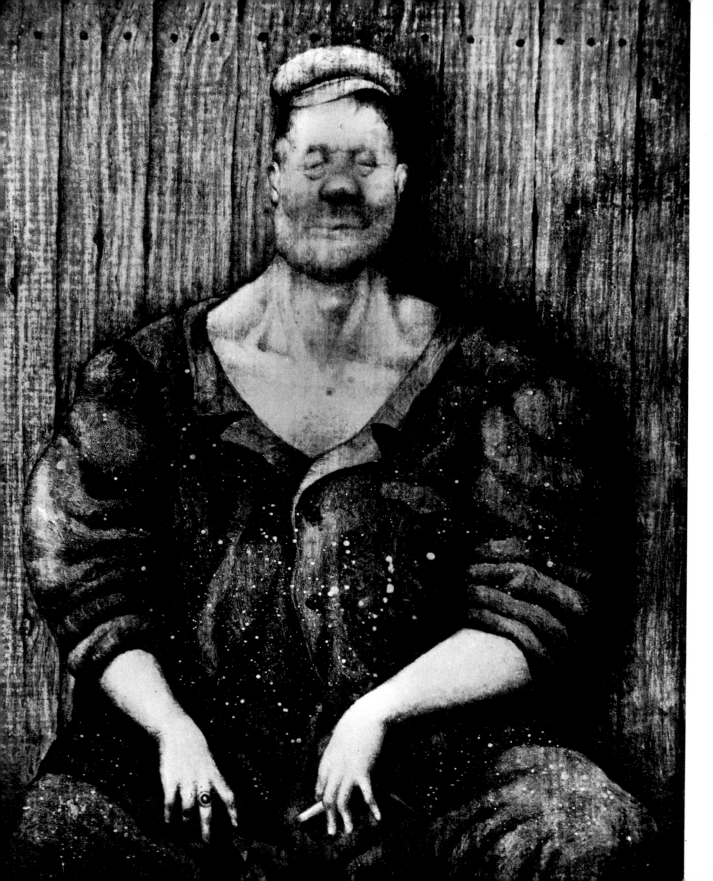

8. Portrait of a Sick Specialist, 1973
9. Portrait of a Critic (J. Waldorff), 1973

10. Venus of Wełnowiec, 1974
11. Two Generations, 1974

12. Homage to Józef Chełmoński, 1974

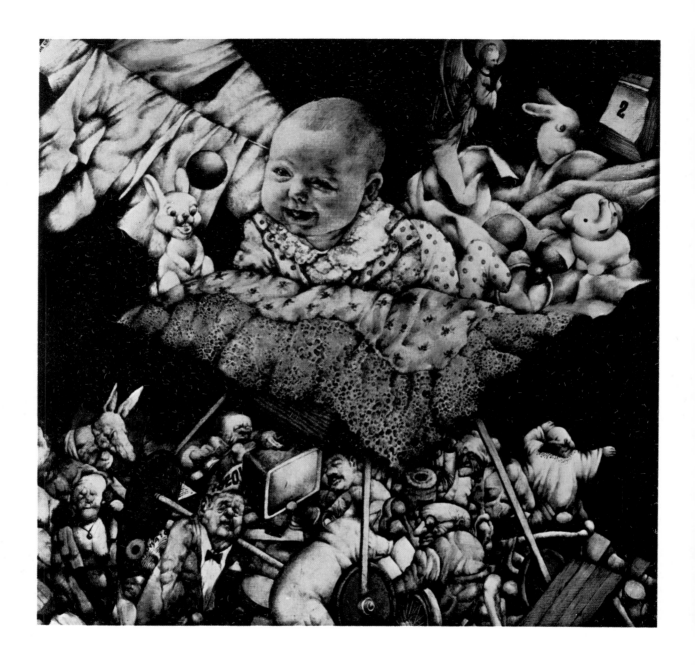

13. Welcome, Little Daughter, 1974

cottages and suburbs with a view of not so much changing their life as creating inconceivable 20th-century structures beyond their framework. Just like the peasants in Bryll's sonnet "still immersed in the shrubbery of the night" and therefore absent from the carriage the are literally in, the protagonists of Duda-Gracz's paintings are absent from the field of their activity. Their attitude is escapism. Into dreams, chats among the rubble of would-be edifices, into the strange delusions of the *Hamlet of the Fields* or poor Bacchic visions. Even the eyes of the *Beautiful Pipe Fitter* escape somewhere beyond the frames of the painting, away from the pipes, tins and wire that form the background against which his pretentious brigand's beauty is shown; even the *Sick Specialist* demonstrates his feminine hands in rings to show that he does not really belong to his trade. They are products of a social shock. It may well be that calling Jerzy Duda-Gracz a painter of alienated people would raise some eyebrows because of the boisterous, at times sly faces of his models, but I cannot resist saying it. Alienation does not necessarily imply a nostalgic tone; it consists in the inadaptability of one's psyche and attitude to one's condition and function, to the reality in which one is immersed. By contrast, let us have a look at three portraits of people from the Tatra Mts, Father, Son and Mother. They are all organically linked with their social status and condition. The background is no longer disturbingly chaotic, the detail has grown pure. The space of these paintings is enclosed within the wooden walls of the house with their rigorous, geometric rhythm. The centrally placed figures are stable and almost hieratic; especially the Son seems to grow from the texture of the planks, their rough uniform substance. A Tatra husbandman lives in accord with nature; those dressed up in dispossessed kings' quilted jackets and undershirts live an unsteady, absurd life. They strive to defend themselves against the absurd with their attitudes, gestures, grimaces and even an apparent docility that conceals abysmal irony, as in the *Concert* where a workman waits for a virtuoso to start his performance. Besides the three Tatra portraits, an organic link between the characters and their condition may be sensed in the series on Hungarian motifs. It is not the right place to attempt an explanation of the phenomenon. Genuine folklore is an historically conditioned trait of the culture of Hungarians surrounded by a sea of ethnically alien Slav nations, and subjected to external cultural domination especially during the period of Austria-Hungary. This has been the mainstay of their national identity, and this is why folk art motifs, elsewhere elements of a carnival masquerade or sham are genuine in Hungarian culture, which is evident in various examples of Hungarian literature and film. The Hungarian motifs in Duda-Gracz confirm the impression: there is nothig panicky in their decorative wealth, at times seasoned with kind wit, a sign of the unity of man and his existence.

I have analysed at length the social reality in Duda-Gracz's painting because I think that it accounts for the public's violent impulses of identification, at times full of approval at other times of rancour. The colossal refuse heap of the endless building plots makes us realise our material surrondings. Our awareness of the mental condition of the soporific province prompted towards urbanisation and industrialisation, the effects of which are felt only indirectly, often through waste material, makes many people in Poland realise their social condition. This may seem oversimplified but evidently what lay behind the social unrest that swept Poland in 1980 was the inconsistency of content and decorum, labour and its effects, the idea of transformation and the stagnation of daily life. It would be an exaggeration to say that as a painter and satirist, Duda-Gracz has carried out an analysis of Polish society

14. Souvenir of a Preventorium, 1977
15. Souvenir of a Solarium, 1977
16. Souvenir of a Sanatorium, 1977

comparable to that carried out by Goya who showed the inner structure, not only phenomena in his contemporary Spain. We may even say that the striving to analyse structure is perhaps the most evident trait of the set of paintings presented. Above the world of the wretched and the humiliated, there is an indefinite world of the haughty and well-fed with something rather sketchy in its outline. This world is usually represented by fat petty bourgeois monsters reminiscent of the synthetic portraits of exploiters in Linke's prints and Heartfield's and Berman's photocollages, and by licentious hags in revolting neglige. The approach is rarely as apt and innovative as the social portrait that we find in the bottom part of the *Polish Triptych*, the irony of which is enhanced by its reference to Kowarski's well-known painting. Instead of the well-defined characters and fresh insights, so powerful in the *Concert*, *Sick Specialist* and many other paintings of people from the "lower depths", we have symbols in the paintings of people "at the top". Yet the appeal of Duda-Gracz's painting and the emotional response it prompts, going far beyond what is usually experienced in exhibition rooms, depends on the forcefulness of its social portraiture.

Does the above statement exhaust the problems underlying Duda-Gracz's art? I think that both yes and no. Yes, because the impact of his work depends first and foremost on the intensity of its social characteristics. No, because we have so far left out of account the part of it which, though evidently linked with the mainstream, the social trend, may easily be singled out not on the ground of its subject matter, intimate and psychological, rather than responding to the anxieties of the industrial world, but, to some extent, on that of its form. I have in mind paintings like the *Portrait of Mme D.*, *Triptych or Trio*, *Agony of Iwona K.*, *Souvenirs of the Sanatorium*, *Preventorium* and *Solarium*, *Forest Nymph*, and in general the trend running through all Duda-Gracz's oeuvre. Here, direct social satire leaves room for more reflective description and more existential subjects. The artist no longer focuses on typical characteristics, and no longer produces something like group portraits of phenomena and attitudes, but on individual types rooted in their community inasmuch as all things human are rooted in it, and at the same time rooted in their private existence and grappling with their individual human histories.

But this introduces another set of controversies about Duda-Gracz's work and creative attitude. We have already discussed limits to the procedure of moral and social unmasking. Now it is time we considered his formal approach. Duda-Gracz deliberately provokes controversy by setting so much store by the distinctness of his attitude as a painter, having nothing in common with the rest of the painting community.

Stanisław Witkiewicz, whom I quoted above, wrote in his *Sztuka i krytyka u nas* (*Our Art and Art Criticism*): "Painting... has encompassed an enormous range of creation, everything that amounts to shape, colour and light in nature, and everything in the human being that can be expressed by means of light, colour and shape."

The other controversy takes the programme of painting as an art basically analysing the matter of the world, put forward by Witkiewicz, as its starting point. Despite the evolution of views of painting since the time of Witkiewicz, both among artists and critics, the view that the goal of painting is to investigate – in this way or other – into the matter of the world or, to adopt a creationist standpoint, the creation of new matter is firmly established. According to these premises, a man and an anecdote fixed on a canvas are painting inasmuch as they are expressed "by means of light, colour and shape", i.e., inasmuch as they fit in with a painterly

28

analysis of the visible world as opposed to "literary" or "graphic" descriptions. Considered from this point of view, Duda-Gracz's painting is blamed for being excessively literary or too much in the nature of prints. Critics insist that neither colour nor light are among the means of expression constituting the artistic essence of Duda-Gracz's paintings, and his use of a brush rather than a pencil or ink is of secondary importance. These charges seem all the more grounded as several if not a dozen-odd of Duda-Gracz's works, including the well-known replica of Chełmoński's *Indian Summer*, also circulate in the form of lithographs impressed by the artist, in which form they have retained their expression and basic meaning. Thus viewed, Duda-Gracz is merely a cartoonist who uses oil paints and a brush, and his artistic procedure is "impure" because he gives his "cartoons" the form of paintings, by which he misleads the spectator into believing that there are certain formal problems in his paintings that are in fact, absent from them. Those viewing the thing from the opposite direction, i.e. painting proper, say that to introduce lampoons into easel paintings and caricature onto canvas is an illicit short-cut taken with a view to sacrificing important painting problems for the sake of communicativeness, that it is all claptrap.

The controversy that I am trying to outline here is difficult to settle. Since the introduction of collages as a legitimate painting procedure, with all the consequences of the breakthrough, the concepts of "a pure painting" or "pure painting" have become almost impossible to define. Using examples of contemporary prints and drawings, in that also Polish cartoons, we may show to what extent satirical drawings, however unpretentious they may appear, have incorporated more and more formal problems, traditionally reserved for painting, as is the case with Andrzej Czeczot among others.

Without going too far in the dispute, I believe that some questions should not be left out of account. What does the substance of the world in Duda-Gracz's paintings look like? What is the world built of? What metamorphoses does it undergo? What are the relations between the material world and the people that inhabit it? In a word, how can the "inconsistency" for which the artist is blamed, be explained in terms of the immanent inner logic of his work and his vision of the world? To what extent is it consistent with his vision?

Before asking the questions, I deliberately referred to painting in which the satirical vein or, if you prefer, the social message is somewhat subdued so that the problems peculiar to painting are all the more visible.

To understand these paintings, it would be a good thing to recall Bruno Schulz and especially an excerpt from his *Sklepy cynamonowe (Cinnamon Shops)*, full of sensual madness, where Schulz describes a thistle-grown rubbish heap with the bed of an imbecile girl, Tłuja, on it. "On these shoulders of the garden (Schulz writes), the slovenly feminine lusciousness of August had swollen into the hollows of enormous burdocks, rampant in their sheets of hairy leaves, luxuriant toungues of fleshy autumn. There, the bulging burdock pudges gaped like women with their legs wide apart, half engulfed by their frantic skirts. There, the garden sold the cheapest groats of elder, the coarse soap-smelling grit of plantain, the wild aqua-vitae of mint and all the worst August trash. But on the other side of the fence, behind the lair of summer in which the idiocy of imbecile weeds had grown rampant, was a thistle-grown rubbish heap. No one knew that there August celebrated its great pagan orgy this summer. On the rubbish heap, resting against the fence and overgrown with elder, stood the bed of Tłuja, the imbecile girl. This was what we all called her. On the heap of garbage and refuse, old pots, 29

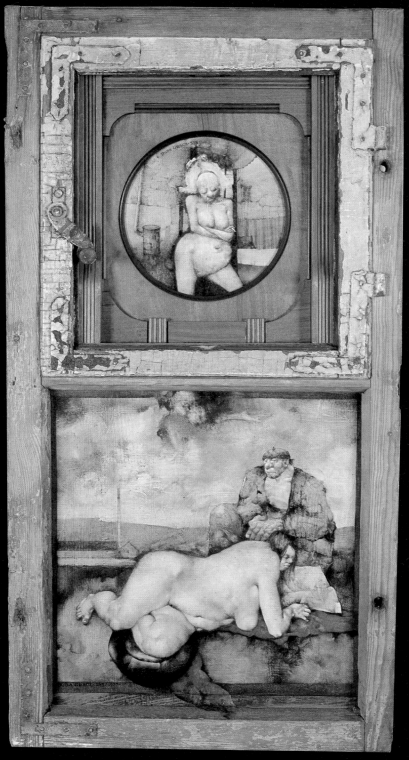

17. Paradise Diptych, 1977
18. Hamlet of the Fields, 1977

19, 20. Babel 2, 1977 (detail and whole)

shoes, debris and rubble stood a green painted bed, resting, instead of on a missing leg, on two bricks... Tłuja is squatting amidst the yellow bedding and rags. Her big head bristles up with a wisp of black hair. Her face contracts like the bellows of an old accordion. Every moment a tearful grimace folds the accordion into a thousand horizontal pleats while surprise stretches it back, smoothes out the folds, uncovers the slits of her small eyes and moist gums with yellow teeth under her snouty, fleshy lip''.

I could go on quoting the description quite unparalleled in its almost palpable substantiality, but I think that what I have quoted is enough to convey the inner logic of the passage. The exceedingly meticulous, almost botanical description of the weeds growing on the rubbish heap results in gradual anthropomorphisation. The intensity and lusciousness of the alder, mint and plantain suddenly bring out the "idiocy of imbecile weeds". The "idiocy" of the untamed vegetation and its shamelessness culminate in Tłuja, the idiot girl living on the garbage heap. She seems to be an extension to and a product of the orgy of the autumnal nature round her, its caricature coping. The plant forms seem to have changed into a human figure, monstrous and androgynous in the sense that her human traits seem to stem from the madness of the vegetation, and her idiocy mocks the exuberance of nature.

I am not saying that Duda-Gracz deliberately follows in Schulz's footsteps though there certainly are points of convergence between the two creative attitudes, for instance, in the intentional provinciality and the sensual outlook on realities. For instance, one look at the *Souvenir of a Sanatorium*, the penetrating *Triptych* or the *Portrait of Mme D.* tells us that they are governed by the same dialectics of causality as that manifested by Schulz. The meticulously drawn forest landscape in the *Souvenir of a Sanatorium* imperceptibly penetrates the old woman's closest surroundings. The walking stick by her chair is part of the forest in addition to being a utility object; her hands have the knotty texture of boughs. The stone wall in the *Triptych* suddenly grows softer on the man's nude back and his hand apparently grows from the mouldy texture of the wall. People are therefore almost literally offshoots of the matter round them, an extension to it; they are the most distinct swellings of it but they are basically homogeneous with the background, as Tłuja is in essence homogeneous with the rampant matter of the vegetable garbage.

Again, as in Schulz, Duda-Gracz's man may be a parody of his environment. In the *Souvenir of a Preventorium*, we see a rocky landscape with the perspective running inwards, as in Dutch paintings. The girl with a candle in her hand shown in the foreground upsets the aesthetic order of the landscape, its conventional beauty. The provocative ovally shaped nude in the *Souvenir of a Solarium* defies the ominous, wild landscape. We have two kinds of relation between man and nature, one is that of growth, the emergence of man from the substance of nature; the other is that of defiance. Both lead in effect to equally parodic forms. The former reduces our human dignity to the level of biological existence; the latter brings out our pretensions and cheap gestures and attitudes in contrast to the solemnity of nature, viz the self-confidence of the nude female patient or the touching meticulousness with which the girl's dress has been knitted.

In this sense, Duda-Gracz's world is deeply tragic. The cheap, poor material surroundings make it cheap and poor. People immersed in this misery do not develop, but degenerate. Even old age does not introduce signs of experience or wisdom into the lineaments but makes them spongy, changes the body into a knotty mouldy substance like that of rotten mushrooms. Thus

34

mutilated, people are unable to set against the world of nature anything except their prententiousness, the poverty of their culture. The pretentious gesture, so often made by people in Duda-Gracz's paintings, is pathetic like Leśmian's coffin shoes, even at its germinal stage. We are in a vicious circle. The world, poor and with no way out of it, is desperately in search of a way towards light, and apparently at odds with its miserable image. Duda-Gracz could repeat almost verbatim another artist's appeal, equally terrified by the ugliness and misery of his visions.

> Blessed Virgin, you're as wise
> As a garden full of grace,
> Throw at least the faintest light
> At Grochowiak's gloomy verse.

This desperately sought "light" in Duda-Gracz's painting is his gift for satirical caricature. The world in which one cannot find inner harmony and a worthy place, tends towards parody in fear of despair. This mental manipulation is fused with a sense of humour rooted in our tradition. Wit as a defence against despair, as a security exit, is the most frequent form of the Polish sense of humour. Thus perceived, the caricatures in Duda-Gracz's canvases, however "jarring" from the viewpoint of the traditional art of painting, spring logically from the philosophy of this art which would be penetratingly sad if it were not for the spontaneous parody and satire that make it so strangely serene.

Krzysztof Teodor Toeplitz

21. Riders of the Apocalypse or Moonlighting, 1977

22. Triptych or Trio, 1978
23. Concert, 1978

24, 25. Top, 1978 (detail and whole)

Entries in the visitors' books of the Touring Exhibition of Paintings, 1978–80

Bravo Duda. Keep up the tune.

Marek

No anaesthetics.

Renata

Superb but unpleasant. Pity.

Signature illegible

Stupid awkward painting.

Paweł Kwiek

So much realism in ugliness.

Andrzej

Foul art from the gutter.

No signature

I thank you, Duda, with all my heart.

Signature illegible

It hurts, Sir.

Anna Gilewska

Protect your eyes.

Rybiak

Your pictures are OK. If I had some money, I'd buy some and give them to my friends. If they had no sense of humour they'd kick the bucket right away.

Andrzej Krajewski manual worker

I think that your paintings are hideous and disgusting.

Ania

It's so true, it's so sad... But you still like people!

Jerzy and Barbara Staklicz

Interesting subjects, hopeless form. Rubens would turn in his grave.

Signature illegible

Mr Duda-G... When will you get into the authorities' bad books?

14.02.79 Paweł Ralle

Hideous filth. (Spelling mistake in the Polish original)

Signature illegible

God bless you! Another step forwards, perhaps?

Signature illegible

Plain truth!

Jerzewski

You criticise everything, but you haven't made the effort to show the way out.

Lay person K.L.

We don't feel in the least offended. But we feel, Master, that nothing can offend you.

S. Klimas and A. Zawacka

My soul is pure again.

Kawajze Filidardiss (Greece)

43

These paintings say more about our society than sociological treatises.

Signatures illegible

Mr Jórek Dóda-Graczó, This is what your painting is like. (Spelling mistakes in the artist's first, middle and second names)

Kłonica of Waplewo

Jesus!!! It's my third visit to the exhibition, but not the last one.

M. Aleksiejew

Real life. Pure socialist realism. Caricature and parody. Cosmic disaster.

Signature illegible

"Duda" is a complete orchestra. Superb, but have the "Riders of the Apocalypse" seen it? Have those at the "Top"!

W. Kalinowski

Optimistic after all.

J.K.

Aren't there too many dirty souls? The exhibition has filled me with disgust at people.

Signature illegible

Gee, it's good!

Employee Aleksandrowicz

Hopeless.

Andrzej of Lublin

Dirty and hopeless!!! Is the world really so grim and ugly? There's nothing to set eyes on!!! Having seen the show one doesn't feel like living.

Girls

My head is swirling and I feel the throbbing of my blood. I am frightened. Your painting is overwhelming but I thank you nevertheless. I am running out to the street, my first aid now.

Majka Z.

I like the exhibition and would like to paint like you. I am in grade 3 my name is Marcin and I go to school No. 6 in Lublin.

Thanks!
You have said what literature can't.

Stanisław Szewczyk

The exhibition is past all expectations. I live in Istebna No. 175. I will come again and again to admire your "MASTERPIECES".

Junoszek Antoni Istebna 175

Mr Gracz,
It's only "Moonlighting".

Signature illegible

More paintings of this kind!

Model from Wrocław

What does the censorship say to this?

XX

Artist! We are all models in your studio. But not all of us are aware of it.

Signature illegible

What you do is NEEDED.

Signature illegible

I feel awkward because I am a worker.

Andrzej

45

Duda, you are good but won't do anything on your own. You won't change "Poles". But go on and do even better.

M. Kuśniewski

All paintings are hideous, the figures are distorted. Exaggeration, grotesque, distorting mirror, nightmare. But why is it all so painfully true?

Visitor

Perhaps someone will understand you in a few centuries. For the time being, I think that what you do is absurd.

Disappointed visitor

If you are like your paintings, I am glad I don't know you.

Signature illegible

Finally a show at which one may and has to, think and draw conclusions and not just run about. I am full of respect for your talent and works. I am leaving deeply moved, not indifferent as I have often been. Thanks.

Signature illegible

You are simply a genius! The reality of your painting is our reality (I am also a painter but too old to learn from you because I have already graduated from the Academy...) All the best.

Barbara Akelbeldt

I follow your exhibition where I can and haven't had enough.

Grażyna Derlag

We have been forced to come to the show with the whole class and now don't want to leave without at least one picture. What you have shown is really superb. We appreciate your courage and the truth you have shown in the best possible way, through mockery. Thanks!!!

Secondary art school students, Jacek Panuś and Lesław Stawski

Pity you are right.

Signature illegible

46

I am twenty-four. Your paintings give me a beautiful vision of the future. Damn!

W. Haser

A good ophthalmic surgeon and a skilful analyst (not and American one) may heal your imagination.

Signature illegible

I have seen the paintings and our Gorzów community painting on the walls with a thick brush for big money. I am furious. I am leaving to come back.

Rutkowski

Are you Christian?

T.M.

Ghastly! The artist has a perverse mind!

Signature illegible

Thanks very much.
Theatre of the Eighth Day, Poznań.

Dear Master,
I admire you for your splendid painting and respect you for the truth you tell. The exhibition is superb. It works like a hot refreshing bath.

Regina Siemieńska

I had long looked at the paintings but have missed something all the time until I saw the *Self-portrait with Family*. That was it. We all fight against the things that you show, but we are all the same, and no one can really fight oneself. There is much optimism in your picking it up.

Marzena Spychalska

I feel like crying! Are we all going to become like this? People are beautiful even when they are old, fat and lustful. They were young too, weren't they? Pity you give no prescriptions!

M. Rodoż

(47)

26, 27. Lower Depths, 1978 detail and whole

30. Level or a Fest at K., 1978

Excerpts from reviews

One of the subtler, though not infrequently met, perverted charms of the art of our time is the love of what only recently was the object of contempt of up to date aestheticians. I refer to the tapestry with the stag, the view with the pond, bridge and a swan, the wedding picture with the groom and the bride in her bridal veil sitting stiffly.

For the avant-garde these were the epitome of bad taste (because not based on mathematical principles) and suspect sentimentalism. For modern artists, not inspired by holy zeal as were the artists of the classical avant-garde, this provincial taste in art offered a marvelous occasion to embroider perfidiously naive pictures.

Jerzy Duda-Gracz paints in the convention of the wedding picture and the embroidered scene of provincial life: the houses are small, the people simple, the rooms dotted with garish wallpaper designs and hung with pictures in oval frames. But this world does not satisfy the artist. Mysterious and terrible faces peak out of the decorations of the small-town theater. In pictures which by their texture and line recall the works of amateurs and in the design on the kilim in front of the bed, we see crawling crabs, flying insects, creatures which have a vaguely symbolic allusion. In one of the works of Duda-Gracz, an old man appears in multiple form, his horrible wrinkled face gazing blindly ahead, and four times disturbs the modern principles of composition in painted and Pop art.

The avant-garde artists were afraid of sentimentality, lest it should erode and destroy the hard building of Modern Life. It does not seem, however, that the present interest shown in the world of provincial charms could inundate the world with sentimentalism and emotionalism. Artists like Jerzy Duda-Gracz have an aesthetic aloofness to the observed and captured conventions. With a gesture that is not devoid of coquetry they invite us to take part in a game.

Andrzej Osęka, *Provincial Charm*, "Polska", 1971, No. 8 ("Poland", Oct. 1971)

Jerzy Duda-Gracz belongs to the group of the most popular and valued draughtsmen of the young generation whose trenchant humour in caricature over the last few years has become a characteristic manifestation in our young graphic art. But it so happens that Duda-Gracz is equally exccellent purely as a painter. That Duda-Gracz's painting is an unusual manifestation on Polish ground primarily results from the fact that his merits as a painter are blended with the dispassionate, penetrative and biting glance of a humourist who encompasses by no means the marginal matters of life, but occurrences in which the dull daily rhythm of life is stripped of all its most typical guises. Jerzy Duda-Gracz has settled permanently in Katowice and has shown his work several times in the "Katowice" Gallery, renowned for the fact that it has launched many leading artists, not only of the middle generation. Among the galleries in Poland which might be called independent, this one has sometimes been the most self-contained and courageous of them all, formulating as it does its own policy, irrespectively of the fluctuations in world art. It is also worth bearing in mind that fact that in the Katowice milieu there was not such an active resistance as, for instance, in Warsaw and Cracow, to an association with the fine – by its very nature – pictorial art with a vision of reality bordering on banality which possibly has its closest counterpart in the sphere of the German Verism in the 1920s. This resistance should likewise be taken into account when tracing the course of the development of 20th century Polish art. It is also necessary to recall that this artist's home-town is Częstochowa which, as a specific pot-pourri of Polish provincialism, afforded the spectacle of the antiquated, the ceremonial and the ecclesiastical purple; a world apart in which the shooting of Fellini's fascination with Rome could have been successfully transferred to a Polish location.

The character of Duda-Gracz's paintings is differentiated. In a few of them a dark colouring predominates reducing them almost to photographs; in others the artist's pictorial technique is a pastiche of the art of the Old Masters, and there is another group – perhaps the most numerous – in which the personal and original gist of this artist's painting is obtained completely in a highly consistent manner. The technique is traditional, but elaborated and intricate in its pictorial structure. While the way of indicating distance frequently used by the artist is aligned to the tradition to amuse, nonetheless it interests him mainly as a device to shift the colouristic handling towards a uniformity in a particular tone, and is decidedly unlike any of the procedures of the traditional painter.

On Duda-Gracz's paintings the graphic and thematic drift of the compositions (the majority of which has been faithfully rendered in a lithographic version), there generally appear the solitary figures of elderly ladies, spectral old gentlemen, the ecclesiastical purples, young artists, the dreams of the country lad, the nightmarish paradise of the smug little house with a garden, and lyrical peeps at lovers. But possibly only a Polish viewer will be able to fully understand the bite of this artist's satirical glance when he compared the country maiden reclining on a lawn with Józef Chełmoński's sentimental composition *Indian Summer* (*Babie lato*), so popular in Poland.

(translated by Doreen Potworowska)
Wojciech Guyski, *On Provincial Motifs*, "Projekt", 1975, No. 1

...Jerzy Duda-Gracz's painting is characteristic on the one hand for its "literary" quality, on the other for its world of degraded values, fetishism, vulgarity. These certainly are not make-believe forms of obscurantism meant to shock the public, but ones observed in the definite world, in the definite social circumstances.

Roughly speaking, the artist observes the middle-class world (which naturally does not imply a social group but mentality); further, he translates many popular fetishes, customs and even a certain type of religiousness into images.

As an artist he is uncompromising to the point of cruelty, but he is just in the flogging he gives people according to their "merits", whether they are equal or "more equal", whether they are on this or the other side of the barricade.

Although his outlook on the world was precisely defined even at his first exhibitions, his means of artistic expression have evidently evolved from anecdotal metaphor (e.g. in *Career Is*

Open) to characterisation by means of visual forms (cf. his replica of the *Members of the Proletariat Party*), to point out just one range of subjects...

Stanisław Piskor, *Jerzy Duda-Gracz*, "Poglądy", 1975, No. 12

...My first impression is that we are dealing with an artistic personality far removed from popular notions; that what has come to the surface with his art makes us look from a different angle at the purpose of artistic endeavours – which approach has long been considered dated – and at the final product of his work, a painting. This new element is literally a story-telling quality which no other medium can replace. Here the artist's personality is visible to the naked eye; it does not address us from behind a painting but somehow contributes to it. Duda-Gracz is not a Don Quixote to undertake things bound to failure; he is not a maniac mixed up with the present, and he is certainly not ignorant of what is going on in art at home and elsewhere, of the moods and kinds of experiment that are over and done with by general accord. Among these is what we see at first glance in his painting, the anecdotal quality. Aware of all this, he comes in with his painting, or his trade, or his production plans, or whatever he and others like to call it, as if nothing happened. Ostensibly, he does not want to be wiser than the public, which is in itself quite unusual here. He has certainly put on a mask, pretends to be a simpleton, has nothing to do with the great ones, he was born in Częstochowa and works in Katowice. His daily effort results in extremely spontaneous pieces, which is another unusual thing. I have a feeling that the success or failure of Duda-Gracz's painting does not lie in the perfect solutions presented on his canvases, in the excellent visual "Schlagwort", but in the fact that by means of a canvas, paints and a brush he transports us to an area where reality is so disturbing that it makes us turn to the unreal, where the non-picturesque becomes so offensive that it makes us seek the picturesque in uncongenial settings from which it is usually absent, where a paradox sounds like a sad truth, and good taste is just as satisfying as the title of Bachelor of Fine Arts awarded by Polish Academies.

Andrzej Skoczylas, catalogue introduction, *"Winners of the C.K. Norwid Critics' Award in 1967–76. Jerzy Duda-Gracz"*

...It would be pointless to dissect Duda-Gracz's oeuvre in a methodical way, first and foremost because what the lecturer of the Cracow Academy of Fine Arts paints, belongs to our daily life rather than art proper that has long and with much persistence sought to work out its own value system, a justified and useful procedure, but only to a certain degree. Having stated this, I am not turning a blind eye to the fact that the painter of the broad-hipped *Souvenir of a Solarium* is obviously concerned with the quality of workmanship, has evidenced his familiarity with the problems of old and – let us call it thus – modern art at every step, and is a deliberate creator of his style. Yet such questions are of interest to the critics and artists only. The mass public has whole-heartedly approved of Duda-Gracz's subjects and message, and is probably rather indifferent to all such subtleties.

To experts anxious to manoeuvre all art into the area of intellectual culture, Duda-Gracz's condition is pathetic not to say contemptible. In spite of it, the artist of Katowice has achieved what only very few contemporary artists can boast of: his work is genuinely present in the culture of contemporary Poland, understood as a system of symbols and signs shaping the collective imagination, modes of behaviour and views. Duda-Gracz's painting is well-known

31. Household Nymph, 1978

32. Agony of Iwona K., 1978
33. Forest Nymph, 1978

34. Portrait of Mme D., 1978
35. Grand Finale, 1978

and talked about in various milieux which is evidenced, among other things, by the numerous entries in the visitors' books of his exhibitions. The title of some of his paintings have become part of colloquial speech. I have myself heard someone say: "He is a Hamlet of the fields" in a patronising, ironical tone. Irony, scorn, deformation and the debunking of reality – these are the words with which Duda-Gracz's paintings are most often described. The epithets may be arranged in different order so that the last word comes first as the one which, according to many, corresponds the best to his message. Indeed, the *Hole in the Ground*, *The Riders of the Apocalypse or Moonlighting*, and *Sunday* are sharply outlined portraits of portions of the world in which we live and participate and which, regrettably, have created ourselves on the road towards a better future. Cultural activists should have a careful look at the *Concert*, an oil painting of an extremely self-satisfied and well-fed violinist representing the altruistic milieu of artists, and a man from the building trade who humbly and with a somewhat ambiguous smile anticipates the enchanting sounds.

IJK, *Environs of Art. Hamlet of the Fields and Others*, "Kamena", 1979, No. 21

...His painting, rich in narrative traits, used to show an image of contemporary man, deeply rooted in the realities of daily life, who is most often treated as the symbol of all our common sins, hypocrisy, weakness, stupidity, ugliness.

The piquancy of these revealing, at times even journalistic works, largely resulted from the artist's use of traditional, one is even tempted to say "museum" methods of representation. Duda-Gracz used to treat the world of old painting as an open repository of ready-made forms from which he quite freely picked up Renaissance, Baroque and all other promptings concerning composition, colour and formal principles. At that time, however, his appeal lay primarily in the narrative quality of his works, the brutal unmasking of sham combined with the passionate unveiling of the squalor of the human condition. The purely visual characteristics of his canvases were less discussed.

His characteristic form of expression was understood later, after years of work and new and newer series of paintings. The artist's exceedingly original vision relies both on his keen observation of reality and very peculiar attitude towards the tradition of painting.

It was not as evident in his earlier compositions of provincial life, featuring a crammed, stuffy world, as it is now that he has moved his protagonists onto the broad arena of the complete human experience and placed them within the frames of the famous paintings of that past. Yet he does not produce pastiches of the famous originals, to which he refers in a loose way, at times through the lay-out of his compositions, at other times through the borrowing of an entire section, an allusion to a type or landscape direct enough to make the analogy evident. He operates all the components of an image, the construction of its intricate spatiality and assemblage of several levels of narration by means of a system of frames singling out the successive distances, which makes us think of the problem of image within image, so important today. Yet the message of his painting largely depends on the single device of introducing contemporary characters, situations and properties, today's drunkards and loafers, monstrous women, the whole hideousness of existence, into compositions reminiscent of works admired for centuries. The message apparently defies all the value systems symbolised here by the proud tradition of art. Though artists have long transformed the achievements of the past, they have mostly done so on the level of the structure of their individual works while putting forward new aesthetic problems. Duda-Gracz, on the other hand, has entered the area of semantics, altering meaning and subjecting everything to his cruel, ruthless vision of the world.

His tales would be ghastly indeed if it were not for his omnipresent wit. Though his comedy is black and bitter, pointed with caustic titles, it unveils the comic aspects of the human drama in plain terms and creates an ironical distance. This is probably why Duda-Gracz's painting, born on the borderline of morality play and satire, has such impact.

Wiesława Wierzchowska, catalogue introduction, 1979

Duda-Gracz's painting... is not intended for metaphysical meditation, neither is it created for the sake of recreation or the satisfaction of the eyes. On the surface, it is all journalism. It is pungent, nonconformist, at times cruel in deriding what should be sometimes protected from derision. But rational considerations do not count here. Artistic creation is neither balanced speculation nor directly emotional. It is obsessive. This does not mean that his observation of people, their characters, ways of being and conduct is untrue and mockery unjustified. But his observation is aimed at the hypocrisy and depravity in the manifested human beliefs, customs, adopted models of living and attitudes, all that deserves to be revealed, mocked or condemned.

One trying to interpret Duda-Gracz's painting may have a feeling that the artist is ruthless in stripping mythical traits off what the tradition of many centuries has given the rank of the symbol of human dignity, purity and beauty. All that has been ranked as the most beautiful product of creative human thought in the past and present, become the pattern of spiritual power and the idea of good carried into effect by man. He unveils the wicked, absurd, hypocritical and ugly traits in man. This is evident in religion-related iconography, rituals and customs just as the ideals of beauty and love, the sublimity and depth of Hamlet's question, just as the dignity of old age and work. But is it connected with the present only or does it also embrace the motifs of the past that the artist tackles? Though Duda-Gracz's paintings echo the past of mankind, the holy or sanctified myths seem so deflated and mocked in his work that the result sometimes borders on vulgarity. Whenever his works deal with the present, they pinpoint the hidden human vices, especially two-facedness and the contradiction between purely declarative principles and slogans on the one hand and the actual conduct and attitudes on the other.

This is why a more in-depth analysis shows that he does not aim to fill the public with disgust and desecrate the timeless, sanctified myths and human idols. He passes judgement on the depraved man of our time accused of the damage done to the most precious spiritual values inherited from the past. Thus interpreted, his work presents itself as a consistent programme of edifying journalism. It is the more effective, the more aggressive and drastic the form of representation. Yet despite the ruthlessness and brutality of Duda-Gracz's critical judgement of man, and despite the deliberate triviality of his approach, he sometimes reveals an unexpected impulse, a longing for sentiment and even bucolic lyricism. This is barely noticeable, for instance, in his *Hamlet of the Fields* or *Paradise* where the fat, repugnant figures are shown with a note of soothing sorrow. In this context, mention is also due to the triptych of *Souvenirs of a Preventorium*, *Solarium* and *Sanatorium*. The landscape in the background is treated with tenderness, not just reverence. Painted in toned-down colours and 63 composed with evident concern for the harmonious arrangement of elements in space, it displays the artist's love of nature, fascination with its charms and sensitivity to its atmosphere. The landscape is poetic and lyrical. Placed against this background, the hideous. figures, characterised with perverse piquancy, stand in striking contrast to it. Aware of the disturbing contrast, and perhaps in order to underline the incompatibility between the two differently approached worlds, Duda-Gracz separates one from the other by placing them in two different planar perspectives. The lyrical landscapes remain within the frames of glued lace or illusively painted wooden slats whereas the hideous human figure, shifted ahead of the frame, presents itself to the spectator not in the foreground but even ahead of the foremost plane of the painting.

Perhaps this combination of ambivalent values, accusing ugliness and lyrical beauty, the uncompromisingly unmasking attitude and compassion, a journalist's passion and the purely visual problem of employing two independent planes within a single canvas and an illusive ctreatment of selected portions of an image, will result in unexpected experiments and achievements.

Bożena Kowalska, catalogue introduction, 1979

...By sneaking... with his parodistic pictures of people living here and now, very precisely defined in the present through the properties used, into hackneyed and banal schemas of representation automatically prompting a sequence of associations, often superficial, sentimental and likewise banal, Duda-Gracz compromises two things at one go. One is our notion of ourselves as ones very neatly fitting in with the world; the other is our notion of the world. As a matter of fact, the parody and grotesque of Duda-Gracz's painting are not related to old painting or, more broadly, old culture, but to our notion of it, our anachronism, our claim that we live in a world other than we do and that we are other than we are. So journalism after all? Perhaps not. This attitude was once called moralising, which today sounds dated, even suspect. But perhaps we should reclaim the term. Perhaps it is the most adequate to Jerzy Duda-Gracz's attitude, perhaps it describes it the best of all?

Duda-Gracz appeals to "refined" minds, to people aware of the whole ambiguity and irony of his painting, capable of reading its contexts and the wealth of hidden meaning. It appeals to people aware both of its formal beauty and points of reference to their own judgements and analyses who, as a rule, do not recognise their portraits, their faces, grimaces, gestures and behaviour in them. Duda-Gracz's painting offends people who, though unable to recognise themselves in it, find the discrepancy between things traditionally synonymous with art proper, and the form and message of Duda-Gracz's painting too glaring and too drastic.

I have no doubt that one of Duda-Gracz's intensions is to offend the prevailing tastes, preferences, intellectual and emotional habits surviving by force of inertia. I have no doubt that he wants to show the world in the distorting mirror of people's notions of themselves and their world. I have described his attitude as moralising, which term, though unfashionable and perhaps even found inappropriate in society, I find positive, even very positive. At the same time, I cannot resist the impression that there is something coquettish in this art, that what shows through the ironical grimace is a cajoling smile and a look of intelligence. There is so

64

much of the world as seen from outside; the artist does not model his parodistic grimaces on the people from his immediate surroundings.

I do not know Duda-Gracz personally. I do not know what people he meets, who his friends are, but to me these paintings speak about things apparently very close at hand, a pompous official or a female shop assistant gorgeous in trinkets, but not of our immediate concern. Despite his apparently uncompromising attitude, Duda-Gracz stops with his criticism at the threshold of the world really dear to him in which he actually lives. This results in yet another note of generalisation and superficiality in his moralising.

It is interesting that the content and form of his works are so closely related. What is perceived on the formal plane as a certain flatness and superficiality of pastiche, as competent workmanship devoid of more profound insights, corresponds on the semantic plane to the superficiality of outlook, the choice of showy subjects and an escape from genuinely sharp and uncompromising judgement. Here, lurid form is coupled with lurid content. Everything is skilfully done. Impressive but not really convincing. One finds the ease and the repetitive motifs and concepts (a device rather overused by the artist) quite disturbing. The latter, employed for years now, does not really contribute anything new except providing more and more variants. But this may be deliberate.

I do not think Duda-Gracz cynical in his recycling of the successes he has once scored. I am not against his painting. I am against idealising competent workmanship and satirical insight, against mistaking skill and ingenuity for depth and significance. I do not like the mythology round Duda-Gracz, and I do not think he should be satisfied with it either. Impressive formulas are easy to utter; the danger is that one may easily believe they are true and yield to them.

Magdalena Hniedziewicz, *Pastiche and Journalism*, "Kultura", 1979, No. 35

...What hangs inside the Kordegarda is life pure and simple which has not until now crossed the threshold of art galleries. It hangs and makes grimaces to itself, provocative in its grotesque, refreshingly unflattering image. We have, for instance, a monstrous trio of manual workers in becoming quilted jackets and jaunty caps, the robust survivors of an alcoholic picnic (*Babel*) or another, no less appealing trio harnessed to a concrete-mixer, on their way to an odd job (*The Riders of the Apocalypse or Moonlighting*). Or a heavily made-up lady idle amidst the triumphant nouveau riche warmth (*Household Nymph*). Elsewhere, a drunken company, overwhelmed with happiness, food, drink and lust (*Level*). Or a pair of rickety children coming home after their first Holy Communion (*Sunday I*). Or a senile couple withering in their conjugal bed (*Sunday III*). Or girls in Cracovian outfit, rolling their behinds in the embrace of skipping dodderers in a dancing scene (*Grand Finale*). These pictures require a coarse vocabulary because they are lampoons speaking about things either left out of account for embarrassement or plaintively hinted at despite the nagging presence of such aspects of our contemporary customs and mentality as absenteeism, alcoholism, selfishness, bigotry, primitive chauvinism, popular lower middle class ideals. Yet it would be an error to suspect the painter of *Moonlighting*, *Nymphs* and *Sundays* of a mentor's tone, castigating disdain, cheap didacticism. "They say I fight hackneyed attitudes. But how can I fight hackneyed attitudes with painting?... I find something funny, annoying, touching, and leave traces of it on panel... I search for the right shape with which to speak about little people's little things. I am interested in things within reach of my intellectual and professional competence.

36. Beautiful Pipe Fitter, 1979
37. Polish Motif. Carnival, 1979

DUDA GRACZ · 400/1979 ·

38. Polish Motif. Pipe
1979

39, 40. Polish Motif. Relay Race, 1979 (detail and whole)

This is why I am not trying to say what man is, but I am saying, with an admixture of self-irony, that people among whom I happen to live have definite qualities, flaws, and comic traits, play dirty little tricks, annoy me... In other words, my involvement consists in a fairly clear account of what happens daily here and now even if it may appear of secondary importance at first glance".*

Duda-Gracz holds a distorting mirror to national complexes and rancour, to cheap plebeian traits, thwarted rituals of petrified family tradition, newfangled smugness. His choice of subjects probably results from his former and current address, in the towns of Częstochowa and Katowice, the communities of which have preserved quite peculiar customs, more apparent than in Warsaw, Szczecin or Wrocław where as a result of the more intense migration, customs have blended, grown more homogeneous and lost their local colouring. Judging from the paintings, the painter's temperament is the decisive factor. He is a realist who attaches importance to the sensual, palpable rendering of customs.

His painting certainly abounds in "quasi-satire"; it is often quite burdened with publicism. Yet the form of each of his paintings (though not always with equal success) supports the narrative layer and, which is more important, contributes to his authorial comment, at times mocking, at other times bitter. Duda-Gracz arrives at it thanks to his use of the means of expression peculiar to painting. Among these, mention is due to his characteristic, mannerist deformation of the human figure, also used in portraits. Asked about it, he gave a witty though evasive answer: "Since childhood, I have been given things quite different from those I dreamt of. When I look through the casement of a painting, almost everything looks as if seen through a distorting mirror in a funfair... I smoke, but cigarettes are bad for the health, I have a house but the door does not close properly... I have even distorted my marriage vows. But since childhood I have kept one of my eyes half-open."

The painter has a marked predilection for pastiche that he uses in a very original way, whether with regard to the whole canvases (his *Babel* is a pastiche of Brueghel's *The Tower of Babel*) or compositional arrangement (his *Level* is patterned upon *The Last Supper*, and the *Suppers* of Veronese and Waliszewski, his *Untitled* is a penetrating transposition of the *Crucifixion*) or individual motifs (his *Moonlighting* features the motif of the troika, and his *Paradise* of Ruben's nudes). He shows amazing skill and marked detachment in his imitation of styles, colour-schemes and techniques, revealing much liking for the 16th-century Flemish painters with their respect for detail, value transitions of warm colours, serene landscapes running inwards, and smooth textures. Apart from his evident references to the great painting tradition since the Baroque, Duda-Gracz also transposes patterns originating nearer the present, for instance 19th-century painting (his *Forest Nymph* seems to come directly from a set of illustrations of the Brother Grimm's tales, and the *Household Nymph* and *Sunday III* are characterised by a post-Victorian horror vacui), and, certainly, 20th-century painting (*Grand Finale* is reminiscent of Georg Grosz's works). Yet in order to describe Duda-Gracz's links with contemporary Polish art, we have to employ concepts other than pastiche or imitation of patterns. The painter of *Moonlighting*, *Portrait of Inga K.*, and the untitled lay Crucifixion has reverted to the difficult tradition shaped by Linke, Krawczyk and Hasior. Yet it would be difficult to illustrate the above with definite works, which does not mean that it has been diffidently concealed. On the contrary, it is evident and evidently immanent. "I am proud that I live and work in a period in which Brzozowski and Hasior have lived and worked. To me,

Krawczyk, Wróblewski and Linke were the paragons of genuine experiments and wise connections, and also form. As for Beksiński and Gaj, I simply envy them their excellent workmanship."*

Finally, a few words on Duda-Gracz's frames, the margins of his paintings. They prove his excellent sense of association, even more than the clay heads of cupids superbly incorporated into his canvases (*Concert, Souvenir of a Sanatorium*) or rosaries (*Souvenir of a Preventorium*). The frame of the *Household Nymph*, oval, decorated with stucco work and additionally bordered with lacy golden haberdashery within the field of the painting, is idiotically glamorous. The *Moonlighting* and several other paintings are contained within scratched window frames varying in format, and *Paradise* within a window frame with a casement. The lay Crucifixion is in a gilded frame originally from an altar. This is sometimes lost in description, but this is how he dots his i's and crosses his t's.

* Jerzy Duda-Gracz statements quoted in the text come from two interviews published in the journal "Poglądy" in 1971 and 1976.

Nawojka Cieślińska, Bravo Duda, Keep up the Tune, "Sztuka" 1979, No. 1/6

...What is the reason for the reserve of the artistic and critical milieu and the enthusiasm of the public? Generally speaking, it is an established fact that Duda-Gracz is very keenly aware of the atmosphere of contemporary life and that he succeeds in conveying it in his painting in a very powerful, very adequate and lucid way, thus deflating the sublime art of painting. He was won favour because he is sharp-witted and brave. He has a powerful imagination and keen insight. All this is enough to account for both the reserve and the enthusiasm, giving a true though unfavourable image of aspects of our artistic life, functioning along socialist lines. Jerzy Duda-Gracz's painting is quite a unique phenomenon in Poland as a rather infrequent combination of a noble and pure art with sharp insights of a social or even journalistic nature, which is incompatible with the pro-French orientation of Polish art. Though Duda-Gracz is sincerely convinced of the artist's duty to work for the benefit of the nation and the cure of its ailments, in which he may also employ wit and mockery, his art raises all sorts of objections and is perceived only on its semantic layer, without paying attention to its purely artistic values. The artist is often blamed for deflating art by placing it in such clear and sharp contexts of mundane reality. In Poland, as is usual with pretentious "high societies", the quality of art is often measured in terms of its conceited detachment from reality while in fact day-by-day reality may, and often should, perfectly well go hand in hand with genuine art which springs from the truth of experience and is sensitive to the most painful phenomena and life processes.

Duda-Gracz is an exceedingly Polish painter. But in Poland, more than anywhere else, most of people prefer relishing their glamour to pondering, if only for a while, over themselves and their surroundings in a critical way, to reflecting on the condition of our country though everyone considers oneself the healer. In this respect, the front is consolidated, though it does not manifest itself quite so openly. Woe to those who think otherwise...

At both Warsaw exhibitions, in 1974 and 1978, Duda-Gracz's work presented itself as the only mature artistic proposal with the ambition to provide comprehensive social criticism, and therefore as an exceptional phenomenon standing in sharp contrast to the predominantly aesthetic or individualist and expressionist attitudes in our art. Both exhibitions revealed a broad scale of the artist's painting potentialities, his purely painterly outlook on objects, at times close to the German Neue Sachlichkeit, his excellent, precise and perfidiously masterly technique, his powerful artistic individuality but especially the aesthetic and expressive competence with which he shapes his extraordinary, penetrating images. Pictorial values correspond to the semantic content of his work. Let me underline that the content and meaning of his art perfectly reflect our common experience of reality, and because of it they have become so very popular with and so well interpreted by the public, aware of its pungency, uncompromising approach and directness. His pictures are genuine journalism in their sharp criticism of human mentality, inertia and passivity, in their illustration of situations to which these lead.

His wit is also desperate in the *Riders of the Apocalypse or Moonlighting*, the erection of *Babel-II* (2000), the *Hole in the Ground* employing the motif of Brueghel's *Blind Men*, the provincial version of the *Paradise* that he has seen somewhere in a suburb, paraphrasing the Venetians or the terrifying hideousness of our pathetic *Bacchus* and our contemporary *Nymphs*...

A passionate account of real life, his art is one of the most superb descriptions of the world that have surfaced in various art disciplines in the 1970s.

Wojciech Skrodzki, *The Most Interesting Show of the Year?*, "Więź", 1979, No. 5

...Jerzy Duda-Gracz's world is true to life. His characters are real people though a little deformed. They are not glossed over, not dressed up, and they look the way we would not like to see ourselves because of our conviction that our bodies and minds are worthy of imitation, that they are timeless perfection. The unveiling of qualities we are not proud of, and parts of the body that we cover as less representational is not, in my opinion, an easy and rewarding task. In order to thus see the world and man, one has to abandon the attitude of a great artist who has a mission to perform and whom no one understands and be a normal man, just like Duda-Gracz. This is why Duda-Gracz is so strange.

Some of the pictures at the Olsztyn exhibition were conspicuous for their frames. Rather than frames proper, he used old window frames and casings with metal elements on them. Making things bizarre for no real reason does not lie in Duda-Gracz's character. So why did he do it? Did he think that otherwise these canvases, essential to the whole exhibition, would be overlooked?

A few days before the exhibition had opened to the public, Jerzy Duda-Gracz arrived in Olsztyn to check the condition of the canvases after the hazards of transport and supervise the necessary repairs. Having attended to the works conveying so much respect for the public, the artist disappeared, i.e., went home without opening the exhibition. This is another symptom of Jerzy Duda-Gracz's attitude towards art which should be compared to the baked or half-baked loaves of our daily bread rather than to iced Easter cake.

(BETA), *Painting Pictures*, "Warmia i Mazury", 1979, No. 6

Since December 1978, when an exhibition of Jerzy Duda-Gracz's paintings opened at the Kordegarda Gallery of the Ministry of Culture and Art, it has travelled all through the country. Słupsk, Olsztyn, Kłodzko, Poznań, Cracow, and so on. Everywhere it was looked forward to, perhaps in anticipation of scandal, with the press trying to suppress their giggle, with the

41. A Street in Gliwice, 1980

42. Polish Cross, Queue 2, 1980
43. Polish Cross. Office Whore, 1980

rumours that the thing is well done. It has been received with interest and had a large attendance. The approval of the undertakings of the Katowice artist, expressed in various ways, shows that the kind of art he practises is much in demand in society. Touring exhibitions hark back to the idea of the *peredvizhniki* or instructive shows organised in the 1950s. In this particular case, instead of a group of artists or an institution, we have a single artist who has picked up the "tradition" in an ironical way. The panache with which he puts his programme into practice results from his awareness of the public needs of today, which sensitivity is rare in contemporary artistic practice when the public has no easy life. It is blamed for its chronic ignorance, indifference to the realities of artistic language, and reluctance to undertake the hardships of perception. Rather than perplexing the member of the public, Duda-Gracz uses a generally accessible language, which he has cautiously enriched with tested devices of art known as modern. In the face of the current artistic trends, an artist who decides to be popular is immediately proclaimed a black sheep. This is why Duda-Gracz's popularity is quite peculiar. Not all are enthusiastic about him though the painter evidently seeks to lure and compliment every professional group. And yet we may risk saying that he has more fans than opponents...

His paintings, characteristic for their lucid messages and simple form, are a direct appeal to our common knowledge of life and the world around us. Let us point out another cultural affinity of Duda-Gracz's art, namely, cabaret satire. The link has frequently been observed but never dealt with in detail as if the marriage of painting and cabaret were the most usual thing on earth. I am very much in favour of doing justice to Duda-Gracz's originality and ingenuity. The world that opens to us in his paintings is flat and one-dimensional, low and cheap, and essentially defective. It is funny but in a tragic way. Indeed, Duda-Gracz has a cabaret bent, but the goal of his art should be seen higher than that, which is confirmed by the exhibition under discussion and his artistic plans. It is not enough to indicate the literary kinship between his painting and the output of Grześkowiak, Groński, Kofta and Pietrzak in the cabaret. The peculiar stylisation that Jerzy Duda-Gracz uses to cover up the absence of a metaphysical dimension from his art obscures his aesthetic genre. The stylisation is related to the glossed over façades, the mass-scale sham of Potiomkin villages promoted to the rank of towns, continents and perhaps even worlds. The choice of this peculiar tone has considerably complicated Duda-Gracz's position in artistic life. Attitudes like this have always been received with reserve. People have interpreted them as the lowering of artistic ideals. Opponents of his art refer vaguely to Art, Culture and History (with letters as capital as possible). Duda-Gracz has had a good deal of extremely bad luck because the critics of his art are always ill-disposed or neglectful. Rather than benefitting from the criticism, the artist may, at the most, feel offended.

Duda-Gracz would like his paintings to be received with all the solemnity that works of art deserve. The merriment of the public is not a source of satisfaction to him. He would like to make the viewer aware of the moral message smuggled in the guise of a joke. Duda-Gracz's experiment is interesting. First and foremost, as an attempt at enlivening egalitarian art, at making it free of the pomp of the professional quasi-initiation.

The feeling that the cases presented in his paintings, though familiar, do not concern ourselves, the spectators, is quite disturbing. Generally speaking, they visualise the Evil that they seek to destroy in a magic way, by proxy. We may find it amusing or terrifying to look at, but this does not bring home to us the truth that evil is not an objective being and that it has our face.

We begin to suspect that a sense of humour interferes with moral catharsis. Bearing this in mind, we may unearth layers of meaning in Duda-Gracz's paintings that are inaccessible to superficial perception.

Henryk Waniek, *Duda-Gracz*, "Twórczość", 1979, No. 12

One rarely gets such an opportunity to watch the reaction of the public to pictures at an exhibition. I do not mean private views, at which some people respond to some other people, and at which there are one or two members of the public wandering about, which by no means provides an opportunity to watch reactions.

Jerzy Duda-Gracz's paintings are full of merriment and so is the public, which makes me embarrassed.

Jerzy Duda-Gracz is an engaging painter (the word is hardly ever used today); his works engage the attention of the public, creating an Event. The artist "shares his art with the public like bread".

I am embarrassed. The communion has come about without the critic; he has nothing to do here, he will not earn his bread this time. Unless he affords a feat like throwing himself at the artist's feet and then into the arms of the public or the other way round. That would be great fun because critics are rarely visited by enthusiasm. Therefore an opportunity to give themselves free rein could be a source of moral catharsis and emotional balance. A balanced critic, that's the thing. Enthusiasm... but I have already said that I am embarrassed or out of balance because they (the paintings) and they (the public) evidently enjoy one another. Without me! I know that if I did not look after myself, a lame dog wouldn't. This sense of being superfluous makes me seek a position between them, by way of compensation. And so I am trying to get in-between on the ground that "A hungry dog belives in meat only." (A. Chekhov)

How did the public respond? They were happy. They smiled. They turned their heads, surprised but also satisfied the way people are after a crisp, well-pointed joke, ribald but palatable. The joke was evidently true to life, "to the flesh of life", but not the flesh seated at the story-teller's table. No one felt personally hurt. As usual in a smart company.

Now, the reactions of those "writing" about Duda-Gracz's paintings: "...lampoons speaking about things either left out of account for embarrassement or plaintively hinted at despite the nagging presence of such aspects of our contemporary customs and mentality as absenteeism, alcoholism, selfishness, bigotry, primitive chauvinism, popular lower middle class ideals."

Or: "Duda holds a distorting mirror to the national complexes and rancour, to cheap plebeian traits, thwarted rituals of petrified family tradition, newfangled smugness."

Jerzy Duda-Gracz is a superb painter. He satisfies all those who expect (or have long expected) art to be clear, to convey a lucid message; he commands the respect of those capable of assessing the workmanship and the degree of refinement; he engages the attention of those wishing art and artists to participate actively in day-by-day life. To make the image complete, we should say that his painting is by all means original, that it bears the stamp of his mannerism (I am not using the term in a derogatory sense), that it contains what was once called *Handschrift*.

44. Polish Dance 3, 1981

The words quoted above, which sum the content of Duda-Gracz's paintings, are absolutely true. More than that. They give a grotesque image of the body and soul, seasoned with satire, carnival traits, perversity of depiction, additionally resting on quotations from "high" culture, and ingeniously set. Contrast enhances expression with the result that we have hideousness in mayonnaise decorated with blossom. The artist has translated his observations into a precise visual language; he has given us a provoking, concentrated solution of reality as if his intention were to quicken our vision so that we did something with it or at least stopped pretending that we see nothing. His handling of detail is superb!...

There are too many clothes. Clothes-properties, allegories, symbols. Horrid smug citizens (*Sundays I* to *III*) are all clothes. The children are child-adults, the image and likeness of adults, little caricatures of overfed caricatures, captive and therefore disturbing. The adults are the ideal satiated, fat, dull daddies in Tyrolean hats, and the equally fat gentlemen's ladies, sprinkled with powder and pasted with lipstick against the background of what? – a house with two small windows. Old people? These are in bed, in pyjamas. The grandmother is in a nightcap, with horror vacui around her. All have dull, self-satisfied faces. They are dressed up marionettes. There is also a pug-dog to make the group complete.
Now the clothes. A beret, a quilted uniform, overalls. Familiar? Familiar. Listen Górecki (italics, italics). And there is also the Hamlet of the Fields in a vest.
The ordinary man in the street amounts to a light coat, a brief-case, a shopping-bag. To clothes. It is not life that we see in the paintings, it is opulent theatre, ingeniously designed, with typical costumes. There is often a different theatre within this theatre, for instance *The Wedding*. We have thus come to squaring accounts with national traditions, myths, flaws, but in so doing, we use second-hand properties. And concepts somewhat isolated from reality. Duda-Gracz employs the instrument called "typicality"...
What is perceived as his individuality results from his peculiar deformation of human figures. But this mannerism also leads to unification, to types with equally generalised traits having little to do with the individual...
I find many paintings in Duda-Gracz's oeuvre somewhat cannibalistic. Why is that? Not because he is ruthless, because his mockery is open and cruel, but because he is so cool, because he gives the protagonists of his paintings no chance, he begins by reducing them to a Type and later stigmatises, unswerving in his march to the goal he has set himself. The most important thing is lost in process. I think about the ruthless, cruel paintings of Bosch, Breughel or Goya who nevertheless saw man in a profoundly humane and compassionate way; their grotesque and mockery are ambivalent and therefore cathartic. Their "movement" to the lower depths resulted in the opposite direction, upwards. They buried values prompting their rebirth.
One of the reasons of Duda-Gracz's "failure" along this path is, in my opinion, his attempt at placing Culture above man, which is evident in his over-refined, over-subtle form over-shadowing everything else; in his "quotations", his efforts at enlivening and rendering more topical traditional iconographic motifs undertaken with a view to "lifting" the subject rather than discovered as a timeless one.
One might think that I have brought Jerzy Duda-Gracz to book for his courage in doing a piece of good, moreover, useful job. My criticism does not embrace all his works. Many have come very close to the truth, not only the truth of our reality, but much more profound, touching our

existence as a live nude body, not a dressed up dummy. I mean his *Souvenir of a Preventorium,* *Souvenir of a Solarium,* and *Souvenir of a Sanatorium,* the penetrating *Hole in the Ground* and *Triptych,* the intriguing *Concert,* the painting titled *Pipe* and several others. I repeat again that his Painting as a whole is excellent. But art should not be confused with painting.

There is something awkward in speaking about art (a capital "A" would be even more awkward), today, in a crowd of artists. Duda-Gracz is also aware of it. This knowledge has brought him to strange fallacies. Let me quote two of his statements. "I search for the right shape with which to speak about little people's little things. I am interested in things within reach of my intellectual and professional comptence. This is why. I am not trying to say what man is, but I am saying, with an admixture of self-irony, that people among whom I happen to live have definite qualities, flaws, and comic traits, play dirty little tricks, annoy me... In other words, my involvement consists in a fairly clear account of what happens daily here and now even if it may appear of secondary importance at first glance." (Duda-Gracz is modest when he says "at first glance". M.R.)

He has indicated his masters and traditions he draws on: "Good workmanship, beginning with Breughel, Bosch and Vermeer, and everything that is a source of faith and, which I am not trying to conceal, patterns for imitation, which tells me that concepts like Art, Painting and Beauty have not died out".

There is no balance between these two statements. Duda-Gracz says that he has modest aspirations but he thinks – and knows – that he aims extremely high. My only interest is the consistency of his work. In order to see the whole of it, I had to lift my head very high.

Mirosław Ratajczak, Flesh, "Odra", 1980, No. 3

Henryk Waniek, a Katowice artist and a friend of Jerzy Duda-Gracz's with whom he has frequently had joint exhibitions, wrote about his colleaugue:

"He trusts... that the Earth may miraculously change into the Garden of Eden, and that painting is an important factor of the transformation." (Exhibition catalogue, "Zapiecek" Gallery, Warsaw, 1975)

"It may well be that we shall finally create a world in which tender-hearted people will learn the art of living from other tender-hearted people, in which trains will arrive on time at the stations of destination, and no plaster will drop onto people's heads in newly erected buildings, in which we shall sooner run out of rye vodka than gentle words. Then, perhaps, Jurek's paintings will lose some of their current meaning. Then we may see them as little justified, eccentric caricatures of the world, exotic and heretic apocryphs. For the time being, let us not pretend we are surprised." (Exhibition catalogue, BWA Gallery, Łódź, 1975)

I have quoted two excerpts from Waniek's essays because I have a feeling that he hit the point in his assessment of his friend's work... Indeed, as it appears from Duda-Gracz's paintings, he believes in the effect of art, in the transformations it may cause in morals and manners. Personally, I am sceptical but who knows whether one who has recognised a portrait of oneself among the painter's works will not ponder over oneself and... who knows? Duda-Gracz is a cruel ironist, passionate in his criticism of our national flaws. Though it is not apparent at first glance, there is trust in people in his paintings. The Katowice painter understands human weaknesses, he hates the stupidity and self-admiration manifested in the

48. Self-portrait, 1981

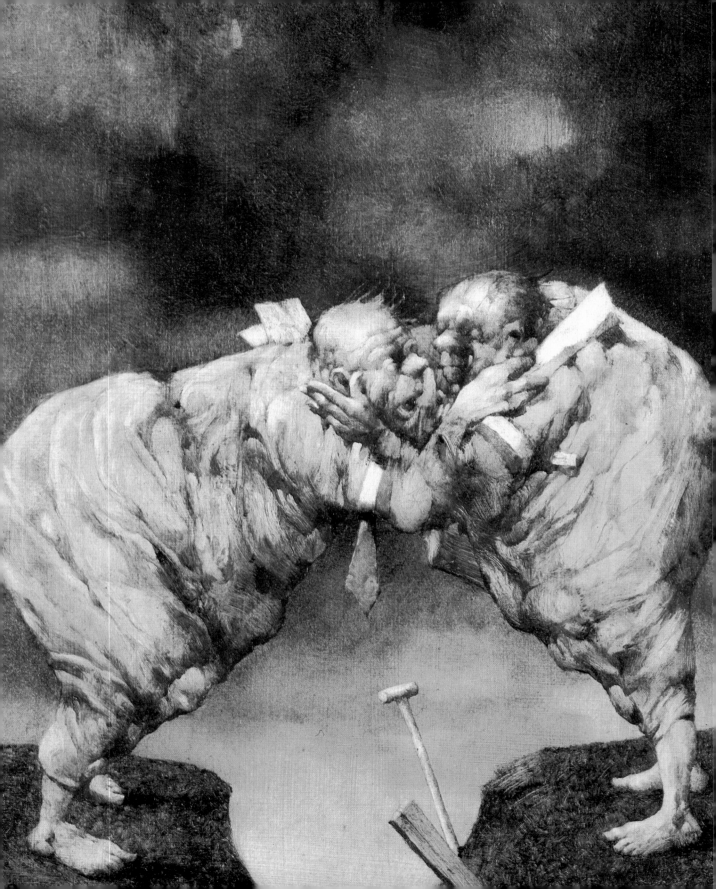

49. Polish Dialogue 5, 1981
50. Polish Calendar 2, 1981

"chum-tu-chum" attitude and sex à la get-together evenings in health resorts. No, Jerzy Duda-Gracz does not deride his heroes. His *Souvenir of a Sanatorium* is a portrait of an emaciated old woman on the brink of the grave, but the scene, cruel in its expression, brands the widespread attitude towards the old, which has made them what they are and caused them to behave in the way they do. Waniek is right. For the time being, let's not pretend we are surprised. When we laugh, let us remember that it is ourselves we are laughing at.

The potential public of these paintings confirms the above. Jerzy Duda-Gracz has said that he wants his paintings to reach private homes rather than museum collections. This accounts for elements of the DESA aesthetics in his paintings. (DESA is an enterprise dealing in works of art and antiques.) I have suspected for some time that this is his concession to the market, to which only the strongest artistic personalities remain indifferent. The public likes Duda-Gracz's painting very much though in many cases the admiration is superficial, without trying to get to the essence of his message. A popular artist always pays a price if he likes to be liked. Duda-Gracz's gratifies the taste of his public a little, by adding certain decorative elements to his paintings, not necessarily justified by the underlying ideas. He knows perfectly well what will make them "gurgle". But I may be wrong, maybe the "DESA" aesthetics is yet another element of the artist's irony; the "camouflage" wrapping may help him smuggle messages which might otherwise by immediately repudiated...

Marceli Bacciarelli, *Let's not Pretend We Are Surprised*, "Fakty", 1980, No. 11

...Disturbing and controversial, exposed to attacks and attacking everybody and everything to show the hideous sides of the human condition. This, at least, is how Duda-Gracz has been labelled. Is it justified? Yes, to some extent. It is certain that all are fascinated by the artist's subject-matter or, to put it differently, his caustic philosophy transforming the world into a disgusting caricature of both his caricatures, i.e. ourselves and himself, and old painting, in which he shows a marked predilection for the classics, beginning with the Renaissance. Very few, however, are aware of Duda-Gracz's form, his brushwork, his tender attitude towards workmanship. It is worth seeing how he grapples with vision, how, by hard work, he gains control of the painted matter and wins in the end. This sense of responsibility for semantic and artistic decisions makes him a direct descendant of moralists like Bosch and Breughel the Elder...

The public will decide what Duda-Gracz is after all. Does he deform things or does he idealise them, does he see ugliness in beauty, does he identify the two or is he unable to separate one from the other? Or does he protest against all the commonplace, wicked and deformed traits in Leibnitz's vision of reality?...

Jerzy Jadeyski Recommends: Jerzy Duda-Gracz, "Gazeta Południowa", 1980, 12 May

...The "Szpilki" weekly brings in its Cracow issue a reproduction of his *Hamlet of the Fields*. I was overhelmed. Is it a new thing or did I overlook it at his exhibition? It compares with Matejko's *Stańczyk*. I regret that, for technical reasons, it cannot be "quoted" here. It is undoubtedly one of the most interesting and the most topical "concepts" of Hamlet. I have been interested in the subject long enough to know what I am saying. Let me attempt a description.

A misty horizon dissects the painting almost in two. Below, there is a swamp desert, above, vapours and clouds of smoke, as in Venus. There is only a glimmer of sun, but it is warm, the earth is enveloped in clouds. There is little air, life is on the decline, but it is still bearable. And there he is, Hamlet enormous and bulky, the only element of importance, like Vrubel's *Demon*. His half-naked torso looms large against the background of the clouds, his legs seem to have grown into the ground. He is old, unshaven, prematurely flaccid. The only relic of his former glamour is his Oxford cap with ribbons and a fencer's muscular arms. But his arms seem vestigial, like a frog's tiny forelegs, compared with the hideous stretch of his fat bulky back, drooping breasts and belly spreading between his knees and sideways in the unbelievably stretched vest with its narrow straps. His trousers, which look like a peasant's trousers, were made a long time ago of excellent fabric, of the kind that stands up to any amount of wear. The settee, which his buttocks fill almost to the brim, has not stood the test of time that well. But it is still his, the only relic of comfort. And there is the skull nearby...

What is our philosopher doing? What becomes a philosopher: he cultivates his garden. He has succeeded in growing twelve miserable cabbage heads on the wasteland. They have come close to his lap, hurry-scurry, like a flock of chickens, and he, leaning above them like a hen, wrinkles his Socratic head, and his pin-like dispirited eyes show tension and sorrow. Will there be enough cabbage until time has come full circle or not? Still he has done his duty as a philosopher, he has made the choice, he has confined his needs, he has made the effort, he has not sought recognition but found it in his own eyes. He has had more reason than others. "What have you been doing?" Sieyés was asked after the downfall of Robespierre. "What?" he answered. "I have survived." Now the only question is: "Will there be enough cabbage?" He still has the cap and the settee, but he also his belly to attend to, his last passion.

Let us shift from cabbage to lettuce, which will give us a tertium comparationis. The Emperor Diocletian, son of a freedman, hence a man promoted to a higher social rank, a good organiser in the spirit of enlightened absolutism, the creator of the cult of the individual (people fell on their faces in front of him and did the like things), known for his doctrinarian undertakings in which he failed, abdicated after a twenty-year reign and settled in Dalmatia, in a suburb of today's Split. "You can't imagine what my patch of lettuce is like," he would say to his guests. In analyses of the life of the scenic Hamlet, little is said about two things that we learn in the cemetery. One is that Hamlet is past thirty, and the other is that there, in the cemetery, after so many experiences which, one might think, have prepared him for the final match, and a new style of living, the eternal student or perhaps doctor, has come back to the question whether there is any point in all this. He says that Alexander the Great, the legendary and the unparalleled, "died... and was buried..., returned to dust..." Like all others. Not a trace of motivation ranging above the individual. Not a trace of gratitude from the descendants or defence of those wronged, and the like. Hamlet has accepted the final match only because of a gentleman's sense of duty to his father and a philosopher's sense of consistency. He has imposed the attitude on himself and literally anything may shake him out of it, for instance Laertes's lamenting over the death of Ophelia. A suspicious psychologist might say that he is on the alert for an excuse, for circumstances beyond control that would justify his departure from the road other than performing his duties to himself. There are good grounds for believing that the Denmark of his father, the Denmark of beer and duties, was a prison to him, and that his prolonged studies abroad were meant to sooth his affliction of heir to the throne. In this respect, Polonius and Hamlet's own affectionate mother were for many years dearer and more gratifying to him. But they "betrayed" him in the end... (There is no need for the Oedipus complex! The complex of a father is quite enough.)

As we see, the diagnosis is different from Goethe's. It is not that Hamlet is unable or unwilling to do things...Certainly, if – in spite of all – his fate had led him to the throne in the end, he would have been a brilliant though controversial ruler, which implies enlightened absolutism, whims, doctrinarianism, and all the unpleasant surprises linked with it. The final praise uttered by Fortinbras is only a propagandist's effect of the new ruler. Here come our questions about the duties of one who has been given a great deal. Brecht asked such questions, and Konrad Swinarski expected Hamlet to answer them. Jerzy Duda-Gracz has asked them in his painting on a broad plane of eschatology. The question is ultimately biblical: "Why have you squandered your talent?" Many of Shakespeare's plays are crypto-morality plays about various cases of worthy and unworthy life. This one is exactly about it.

M.A. Styks, *Hamlet of the Fields*, "Życie Literackie", 1980, No. 34

...Where does the realism of Duda-Gracz's painting lie? I believe that in his rendering of visible reality. Duda is one of the few outstanding artists who paint from nature. Even if his compositions are to some extent surrealist, visionary, and metaphorical, the objective, literal quality rests on his memory of the concrete. We have spoken about the almost extinct species of realistic portrait painters. But Duda paints dozens of ordinary portraits. We have spoken about the species of landscape painters, not extinct, perhaps, but considered of minor importance, mostly on the ground of professional hierarchy. Duda paints landscapes not only in the background of human figures after the Renaissance fashion, but also quite "ordinary" landscapes, just for personal pleasure. He rarely puts them on display, partly out of respect for "real" landscape painters, partly because of the secondary rank of the subject.

But this is an easy way of answering the question. The realism of Duda's paintings lies deeper, in his approach to objects, in his love of facts, bare facts, occurring here and now, in this very place. A fact does not only embrace the construction of the bench on which an old peasant sits, but also the way his legs are crossed under the bench, and the way he has clasped his hands on his lap, all of which the painter has observed with much precision. If there is a difference – at times very small – between the painting and the observed reality, the latter not necessarily depicted from nature (Duda does most of his work in the studio, just as the Old Masters did, and unlike the Impressionists who stuck to the above principle or felt they had to), it lies in his handling of colour. Apart from evidently metaphorical compositions, colour, though deliberately lifelike, is evidently man-made. It is very difficult to describe the glazing, at times succulent, powerful and contrasted, or based on dissonance, at other times, which is more frequent, delicate, transluscent, covering the surface of his paintings like the faded lace that an old bigot has taken off.

...Duda-Gracz first sees the facts which only later arrange themselves in mythical structures. He must have first seen a poorly constructed building (the metaphor of a home should be understood more broadly), and only later did the image prompt the emergence of that of Brueghel's *Tower of Babel*. He must have first seen a girl in plastic boots, with a transistor radio in her hand, minding cows, and the observation prompted his pastiche version of Chełmoński's *Indian Summer*. It may well be that behind the misery and pathos of his *Mountain-Crucifixion* is the image of our brave boys operating a microphone like a sword and a sponge soaked in sour wine, both at a time.

I think that this history of the emergence of mythological motifs in Duda-Gracz's paintings, from observation to metaphor, has its source in the artist's more general attitude. In fact, it testifies to his sense of the peculiar duration of the world into which he was born... But it should not be confused with the naïve faith peculiar to painters of sentimental lowland landscapes or household pieces with a child in the background. Duda-Gracz is too wise, too deliberate for that. He is perfectly aware that the fluidity of the world is more than justified, that morals are out of joint, and so are principles, that politicians have gone daft. His sense of durability is quite peculiar as it embraces stupidity and evil rather than good and order.

... Duda has as much sense of the stability of the world as trust in the endless potentialities of change. Still he ist primarilly a painter of place and time where the durable transforms into undurable. Where the existing comes into contact with the new. The declining with the newly-come. It happens on the broad plane of individual and group life.... This is evident even in the structure of the represented world: almost every other work shows reality consistent in its general outlines but already crumbling in places. For instance, there is a wall, with the plaster cracking or even falling aparat; there is an edifice supported by a makeshift scaffolding or with glaring gaps; there are the faces of smiling children but their complexion and appearance are sickly, rachitic; the "rider of the Apocalypse" has swift legs that urge him to the unknown, but his face shows the effort and weariness of many years. This world is on the borderline of health and sickness, stability and decay. Hardly anything is in place, hardly anything may be trusted. And yet the great Makeshift, the Eternal Transition Difficulties, as if in defiance of common sense and the laws of physics, keep reality alive and, paradoxically, guarantee that what seems on the brink of annihilation is in fact imperishable.

This also applies to paintings where some stereotypes are shattered to leave room for others. Where we see an old peasant in a long greatcoat, striped shirt and a tie, and his son, with a tangle of hair down his arms, in a loose jacket, baggy trousers, and a transistor radio under his arm. Both have the same kindly smile and the same potato-like noses in healthy pink in the middle of their faces.

...Characteristically, Duda-Gracz is almost indifferent to "pure" customs, modes of behaviour, appearances. Something is always contrasted with something else even if the contrast consists in simply putting things together. This is why we do not come across depictions of closed, codified cultures, either urban or rural... Naturally, Duda, a typical representative of "low", plebeian art, is more interested in the suburb than in the city centre, a small town than the time-honoured folklore of poor villagers... He traces coarse faces of the former small-town dwellers in the wearers of smart suits; he traces urban traits and the inspiring presence of a TV set in a peasant cottage; he is not interested in the hippie as such but in a plumber stylised after a hippie; he sees the compact buttocks of an ex-cowgirl under furs, tulles, and lace; he guesses an ordinary country woman, who is a mixture of kitsch and Phoenician ambitions, in an avant-garde lady rigged out in jeans and dollars who has come from a distant world.

He traces natural traits under a period costume; he likes to discover the familiar faces of Grójec or Siemianowice in people who have fixed their gaze on alien patterns and are fashionably

54. Polish Dance 5, 1982

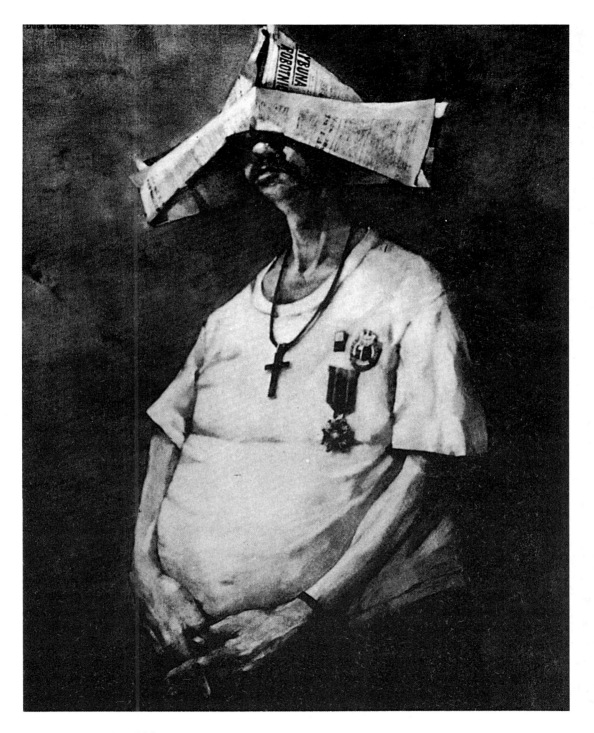

55. Self-portrait, 1982

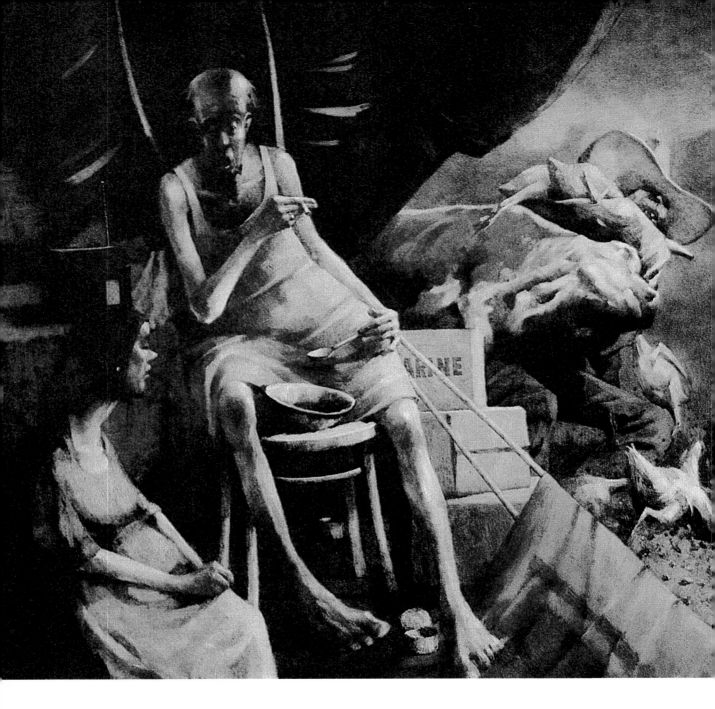

56. Polish Motif with Chicken, 1984
57. Portrait of Wilma, 1983

58. Polish Motif. Exodus
1983

dressed up; he knows that the Polish face and Polish nature cannot easily be uprooted from the thousand-year soil even though time is propitious to such transformations. He also traces kitsch in life stories and in civilisation. He sees people's attempts at covering themselves up behind the cloak of passing snobbishness (even if it is not quite deliberate), yielding to superficial myths, the appearance of truth, the whole mental and existential staffage of our existence as kitsch. But one does not really know where the kitsch starts and ends. The main reason for it is that the artist's answer is not always very clear. I have a feeling that this is not because of ignorance or reluctance to define his stand. Rather, Duda-Gracz often considers the given issue unsettled and does not want to impose his interpretation against facts. How are we to distinguish kitsch in the attitude of an inhabitant of the Tatra Mts who puts up an image of the Virgin Mary among nudes cut out from illustrated weeklies? It is partly funny, partly desecrating, but altogether true to life. The plastic boots worn by a girl minding cows are undoubtedly kitsch, but is a miner's six-year-old son wearing a black Sunday suit, a tie and black pumps on his legs a case of kitsch or an heir to a live cultural tradition?

...Duda-Gracz photographs this merry-go-round on the run; he is anxious not to leave out any important detail of the bitter and often futile play upon life. Now and again, he picks up a delinquent, lifts him from the chaos, watches him attentively and, while documenting the external staffage, tries to look him in the soul. He wants to see the Pole's real face behind the mask, make-up and slogans. This is why Duda's portraits are in fact internal, psychological. Let us not be deceived by appearances when we look at the numerous portraits of apparent simpletons in quilted jackets or the prewar wedding outfits that they usually keep in chests in their cottages: their faces bear many signs of practical wisdom, and Duda-Gracz would be the last person to make fun of his models... In the portrait of a young couple at table covered with all sorts of delicatessen (the painting is titled *Let's Make Ourselves at Home*) we recognise Duda-Gracz and his wife. This provides an answer to another question, about the painter's relation to his protagonists. He simply places himself and his family on equal rights. At times ironically, as in the picture of himself and his wife at table, at other times somewhat perversely, when he portrays himself picking his nose with a brush.

...I believe that there are at least three reasons for the popularity of his works. One is banal. People get what they readily accept as art. Moreover, this kind of art is very similar to that regarded as the European aesthetic canon at least since Michelangelo. Since the canon has been repeatedly defied by 20th-century artists, the public, perhaps prompted by their innate conservatism, like to support what they like or, to be frank, know.

Another reason lies in the area of direct meaning. Duda-Gracz has come close to what Marcin Czerwiński calls the "common public experience" (*Samotność Sztuki – The Loneliness of Art*, Warsaw 1978). At least at the current stage, this experience consists primarily in a kind of individual and group sense of identity. We have already discussed some of its aspects, the struggle between the "new" and the "old" in the area of morals, behaviour and appearance. In this context, it is time we discussed the current state of possession. What we have, what we have acquired, where we are. Here Duda-Gracz focuses on the sore point, on how we exert ourselves to make the most of life, especially materially.

A critic (Mirosław Ratajczak) has rightly observed that Duda paints clothing, properties, our daily little theatre, the cloakroom and the stage at the same time. Indeed, costume is extremely important in Gracz's painting. It is not only the black suit that the miner's son wears or the gold

102

ring on the plumber's finger, but also a Fiat 126p in front of a one-family house, a table strewn with victuals, a motor-cycle handle-bar steered by a peasant "rider of the Apocalypse", and the transistor radio lifted to a cow-girl's ear.

But the documentation is ambiguous. Evidencing our state of possession, quite pathetic to be frank, it unmasks the triviality of the consumption era, which is how the 1970s were planned. Kitsch traits are quite evident. But who knows if it is not in this and many other, quite literal types of kitsch that Duda's public finds a source of peculiar perverse pleasure or quite serious satisfaction.

Finally the third reason, the most evident perhaps. Duda-Gracz presents himself to the craving eyes of the public as one of the very few factographers of the truth about the Polish condition. Among all this winking, lying and contour-blurring, artificial delights and assumed superiority, the blabbery of the mass media and the sloth of art, his work speaks in a human voice. It appeals to consciousness and evidences the courage of living with one's eyes open.

Tadeusz Nyczek, *Photographs from a Merry-go-round (on Jerzy Duda-Gracz)*, "Pismo", 1981, No. 5/6

...Question: Do you consider yourself more of an artist or a craftsman?

Answer: Decisively more of a craftsman because what I value the most is the foundation of workmanship which simply makes the moment of creation easier. Next there are motifs resulting from the choice of the subject, and only later things that may be classified as strictly artistic or formal.

Q.: Provided what you do is art after all, do you consider yourself a painter or a representative of other visual arts?

A.: I would have to consider whether I am a painter, at least in the traditional sense. I think that painting is perceived in a somewhat absurd way today. To me, the stimulus for painting a picture has little to do with painting. This is why I don't necessarily have to call what I do painting. I have always defended myself against calling my output "painting". I call it painting pictures, which is a broader term to me. A painting is a means used to convey ideas.

Q.: You convey ideas through powerful expression or, to put it more bluntly, the deformation of reality. Do you mind if I called your work satire?

A.: I do. I do not think I have ever been a satirist. But I found it quite convenient to be classified as one because the public had access to my works, for instance through papers. I am speaking about the years when I was beginning to paint.

Q.: I have seen your latest works and had the impression that they were satirical because of their content. Perhaps there are grounds for calling your work satirical?

A.: I protest! Those who write about me like to see satirical traits in my paintings for the sake of convenience.

Q.: Since you show our life in a distorting mirror...

A.: Why distorting?

Q.: You are not trying to say that the plumber in overalls, with rings on his fingers is a faithful photograph of reality?

A.: Is a pipe fitter with a lady's hands an image in a distorting mirror? It is objective reality. When an expert comes to me to fix a pipe, he is the one who sits and eats, and I am his errand boy. He sends me to get him beer, vodka, smokes. In the end I do what he should do. I painted him the way I did not for the sake of joking but because that was how I visualized my experience.

Q.: But I have a feeling that you are pulling my leg in denying any link with satire so categorically.

A.: I do so because I would like to avoid what happened to Bronisław Linke to whom, God forbid, I am not trying to compare myself. He showed the terrible drama of people but because he published his works in the "Szpilki" satirical weekly for some time, he was labelled as a cartoonist. Twenty years after the great artist's death his image is still the same.

Q.: How do you comment on the smile with which people look at many of your paintings, and on the fact that each of your works may be described verbally, which you like to do yourself?

A.: I wouldn't object if you called my speaking pictures painted journalism.

Q.: But what kind of journalism, news or comment?

A.: It depends on the situation and my state of mind. What you call "comment" was the right word at the beginning of my work when I thought and felt it my duty to bite. What did I bite, what did I attack for six-eight years? Ignorant of the cause, I attacked the effects. I had to grow internally to tell myself about 1976–7: "Be brave enough to get to the cause." And my painted comments have since changed into serious journalism. But my public and those in charge of classification got used to grinning and so they grin when they look at my paintings even though they are so grim.

Q.: Is it not because of the caricature deformation of the figures?

A.: I only partly agree with you. You see the figures deformed.

Q.: Do you see them "normal"? Or is it subjective artistic vision?

A.: Painters use this expression to protect themselves against the type of questions you keep asking me. They say: "It's the way I see things," but it isn't true. We all see in the same way, and if one doesn't it's because of an eye dysfunction. It is a matter of seeing things with the eyes of the imagination, of temperament and character. This is how I feel about the protagonists of my paintings. I try to show their appearance as objectively as possible and at the same time to denude their inner selves. My moral principles would not allow me to deform people for the sake of fun or mockery. I have never done it.

Q.: And yet, people feel hurt from time to time.

A.: Let me tell you what I have already said on some occasion. There was no coquetry in it though some felt there was. All the people depicted in my paintings, thin and fat, from the Establishment and from the working classes, the nightmarish old ladies, the girls receiving their first Holy Communion, and the characters that made their appearance after 1980 – all these are an endless sequence of self-portraits. I am present in all of these. I, a person conditioned by reality, by situations in which I have been... If there are twenty characters in a painting, I am in each of them, and in the painting as a whole. There is nothing skittish in "deforming" myself. Do you agree?

Q.: Not quite. I don't see you in the pastiche of Chełmoński's *Indian Summer* nor in the painting featuring Lenin and a bourgeois.

A.: But I am there too! For one thing, because of my plebeian predilections, and for another, I feel "bourgeois" as you have put it, because I can sell my paintings privately at the price of a sheepskin coat each. If I paint two figures in a definite relation with each other, for instance

104

59. Jurassic Series, 1984

a party comrade and a cardinal, it is because I am not sure if I do not act according to the principle of "a foot in both camps". In this sense, it is also my self-portrait.

Q.: And when you show the 1980–2 events?

A.: The events prompted my inner conflicts and in this sense the paintings are also my self-portraits.

Q.: I am not going to deny that what you have said is beyond my understanding. I don't know whether there is any point in my next question: Why do you attack working-class people so often?

A.: To begin with, I don't attack anything and anybody. What I do and what you may find caricature or desecration, is an awkward attempt at catching up with reality. It is far beyond me, of which I am growing more and more convinced. We have looked together at the *Polish Cross* that I painted in August 1980. Barely a few months later I felt very clumsy, very unqualified to "grasp" reality and transform it into pictures. As for the working-class motif, it features in my work because after my studies I did not settle in Warsaw or Cracow but stayed on in Katowice. Because my work is founded on experience, I try to speak about things with which I have had contact or which concern me. Hence the working-class motif. As for the journalistic edge of my paintings, it is at the most levelled at myself. I know you may find it improbable, but believe me, I can't create things if I have not carried them within myself.

Q.: Does the public understand better than I what you say about the endless series of self-portraits?

A.: I assure you that while critics, people who write on art by profession, are not aware of it, the visitors to my exhibitions, those who approve of me and those who don't, are.

Q.: How is your art perceived by the ordinary man in the street?

A.: Most people see it as satire but they are conditioned by what they have read. Quite a few, I don't know if I may speak about a majority here, see political and social problems tackled very seriously in my paintings. About 90% of the entries in the visitors' books show that the people are extremely sensitive to the subjects of my paintings. This keen social response proves in my opinion that my works are close to reality.

Q.: Are you pleased with all the entries?

A.: Of course. First and foremost because they express reactions to my work, enthusiasm or a violent refusal to accept. There is nothing worse for an artist than indifference, and this I have been spared.

Q.: What is the source of enthusiasm?

A.: Most often correspondence between the subjects of my painting and reality. Also my workmanship, the fact that I hark back to old painting.

Q.: What are you blamed for?

A.: For the wrong associations that people make. Some get indignant when something reminiscent of the Crucifixion has too many human elements in it and is not sacred enough.

Q.: Is there anything those indignation-prone ones have in common?

A.: They are either very young or very old. I am a little surprised because I understand the reaction of the old, used to a different kind of painting, to a different outlook on reality. I do not understand the young who, judging by their entries, protest against my image of reality. A girl once wrote: "I feel relief because I am about to leave your exhibition and go to the street, to the normal world, to people." There are often entries saying: "You are not normal, you should

60. Jurassic Series, 1984

undergo mental treatment." Thus people of roughly the same generation perceive the world differently.

Q.: How do they treat you during your meetings with the public?

A.: I deliberately do not take part in any meetings and do not hold private views. But once I had something quite like a meeting. In Olsztyn, members of the staff of the Bureau for Art Exhibitions told me: "We are about to close the gallery. You have a quarter of an hour to tell us what your pictures are really about." I didn't think I could tell them more than they could see for themselves. But the meeting lasted three hours. One of the girls said with surprise: "Does it mean that you have all this nightmare on your mind every day? How on earth can you live with it?" I found it very hard to explain that one's self cannot be separated from one's work.

Q.: Preventive psychotherapy would be quite useful, wouldn't it?

A.: Landscape painting is my psychotherapy, of which hardly anyone knows. I started to paint landscapes in 1972. My descriptions of the social reality are much less intense than reality. A documentary film would be much more faithful. And yet, I often feel I have had my fill of both objective and painted reality. When I grow insecure and tired with dissecting day-by-day life, I rush to the mountains. I have my "digs" at my friend's who lives in Brzeg near Bukowina Tatrzańska. This is where I recover my sense of proportion. It is rather banal but I am not going to hide it. Banality quite often runs through my life and work. There, on the bosom of nature, I become aware that I am only present here for a while and begin to ponder whether I should really submit to all the kinds of hysteria that I am trying to record in my paintings.

Q.: Does landscape painting as a relaxation affect the mainstream of your work?

A.: I don't know. But you have seen how my workmanship has changed, how I have given up all the detail, warts, wrinkles and the like. I am more and more convinced that all this is superfluous, that there are much more important things than depicting things in detail. This may be the influence of landscape. The power of nature makes me humble, and it can't be precluded that something of this humility will penetrate my painting of the social reality.

Q.: Aren't you afraid that the evolution will take a different course and you will end up as a realistic landscape painter, which is considered rather banal today.

A.: I don't know what will happen and I don't care at all. I simply have to listen to myself. Before I didn't calculate that it would count to be a "pure" painter to get into books, but wanted to speak through my paintings at all costs, and didn't suspect it would arouse so much interest and cause so much controversy. Neither can I be sure at this moment that I shall not end up as a landscape painter or sink into dotage, which is bound to happen in ten-fifteen years anyway, and start painting light, entertaining pictures that people would call "lovely".

Q.: So far, your painting evolves in the opposite direction: the depicted reality grows uglier and uglier. Does it reflect a similar process in your mind?

A.: As I said, at first I attacked only the effects of definite social circumstances. After 1975, I started to think I shouldn't go on this way and be brave enough to reach the cause, to find out why we were so "ugly", immoral, false. This is why in the late 1970s my paintings grew increasingly drastic.

Q.: But the so-called objective reality was no more drastic in that period than, for instance, in 1970. On the contrary, at the beginning "Poland grew in power, and people were better off."

A.: As you know, that was a myth, and the objective truth was beginning to look somewhat different in about 1976. Besides, the evolution of my art proceeds between two tracks. I record reality in a realistic way but also pass it through the filter of consciousness. I now understand things in a different way, I might have even grown equal to them, which has affected the message and the form of my paintings.

Q.: I think that the secret of their impact lies in your social consciousness coinciding with that of a large part of the public. But how do you see their future as works of art?

A.: Quite grim. First because most of them speak about things that are evident only to us living now, and second because they are burdened with a peculiar kind of regionalism so that only Poles can understand them. After a few years, they may become apocryphs, curiosities. Then they may defend themselves as works of art only through their form or craftsmanship.

Q.: Your pessimism may be slightly exaggerated.

A.: If another Marek Rostworowski is born in a hundred years and puts on another exhibition "The Poles' Own Portrait", he may show my paintings among other works as a document of the period.

Q.: Will they be an "honest" document to those unable to confront the paintings with reality?

A.: To consider the problem, I would have to talk to an expert in the history of art to be able to communicate an assessment of my work to the future generation, or to an editor of the "Mówią Wieki" historical journal rather than an editor of the "Tu i Teraz" weekly. This is a kind of demonstration on my part.

Q.: People say you have never showed your works abroad. Is it a manifestation too?

A.: I do not show my works abroad and I don't care how my work will be received in a few dozen years for similar reasons. I have had much proof that foreigners, even ones worthy of respect for their scholarly titles, understand nothing of my paintings and interpret them in quite the wrong way...

Q.: Nothing new. You must have heard of Matejko's failure at an exhibition in Paris. An outstanding French art critic was interpreting his *Rejtan* as an image of a Polish nobleman who had got drunk at a party, started overthrowing furniture, and finally brought himself down so that the master of the house had to show him out. Matejko heard the explanation from a hiding place and we can imagine what he felt. Are you afraid of similar failure in your contact with the foreign public?

A.: Or even bigger. Though my painting is an appeal for more universal reflection, for considering what we are like, where we have come from and what we are striving for. But in my interpretation these are our internal affairs, which is why these paintings are clear only to people interested in the Polish realities.

Q.: Have you had an offer for an exhibition abroad?

A.: Yes, from the Kościuszko Foundation to have an exhibition in the USA, and other offers for exhibitions in Paris and Switzerland, but I have declined. The prospect of meeting foreigners and the more, so ex-Poles was enough to discourage me.

Q.: Does it mean that you don't leave Poland even as a tourist?

A.: So far, Dresden is the farthest place west I have been. There I could see the originals of two works of my dearest and most faithful ally, Vermeer.

Q.: You could see many more in Paris, Amsterdam or Washington.

A.: My friends encourage me even more energetically. They say: "You live in your cocoon like a silkworm. You sit in your Katowice like a fool. If you went to the West, you would see Poland from the right perspective." I fear that if I went, I would share the lot of those whom I once

61. Jurassic Series, 1984

admired because I thought they would be able to resist the mental pressure of a confrontation like this. But then I found to my regret that they had run out of creative enthusiasm. When I asked them about impressions, they would say, "There is no life here." I think that observing the world from one point only may be as interesting as observing it from outer space. The thing is that one should do this honestly.

Q.: This is an isolated attitude in our post-war art. But the history of Polish painting knows many artists, beginning with Norblin and ending with Sichulski, who practised a genre similar to yours, in some cases only as a side interest. They included as outstanding painters as Orłowski, Michałowski, Kostrzewski, Grottger or Wojtkiewicz. To me, some works by Smokowski or Pęczarski could have been painted in your studio. Are you aware of these connections?

A.: No, it's the first time I have heard this comparison. But connections are a fact because no one comes from nowhere and we are all genetically conditioned. It is impossible to create anything on a surface enclosed within four battens which would not be similar to an existing work at some point.

Q.: Do you feel a closer link with any other Polish painter?

A.: I do, and you'll be surprised to hear with whom. With Jan Matejko. Even when I was a child, Matejko was like a god to me. I read everything I could lay my hands on about him. I found in his letters what years later became my inner need: deliberate abandonment of purely painterly values in favour of conveying a message. Besides, I am just as accurate, you may say neat, in my work.

Q.: What about Matejko's ideology?

A.: Ditto, though in a somewhat perverse way. As we both know, Matejko painted for the encouragement of the hearts. I, on the contrary, pull people down a little. But I am aware that it requires an effort to engage the contemporary spectator in a dialogue. He is used to the strong effects of the mass media, and to horror in the cinema, but in painting, he looks for what he can put above his bed. I want to upset his peace of mind a little because I love him "as I love myself". I do not want him to expect that art is recreation, because it is not the function of art. I do not want him to treat paintings as elements of furniture. My goals may be described as social instruction, which I set above all things spelled with a capital letter, Creation, Art, Painting.

Tadeusz Kucharski, *What's Inside Duda-Gracz*, "Tu i Teraz", 1982, No. 30

...I do not consider myself a painter in the traditional sense of the word because the visual expression of my paintings does not depend on inspirations and problems peculiar to painting, but on semantic and narrative stimuli from beyond painting. To me, the most important thing is the thought, the idea that is behind the meaning and shape of a painting. Form is only a means of expression, not the goal. That's one thing.

Another is that I defend myself against hasty classification, but I am not desperate about it because I trust in the intelligence and sensitivity of people for whom I paint. It is these people, not those who arrange things in classes, who establish the categories of my paintings. For fifteen yers, I have practised "painted journalism", spoken with my paintings about the realities with which I and all those whom I address are stuck that have shaped me and my work, formed me for the benefit of the public, which I have often had an opportunity to see.

Those in charge of classification have summarised my social service with a sequence of labels such as a painter of the provincial life, a satirist, a moralist, a scoffer, an iconoclast, and the epithets resulted from their needs, tastes and circumstances. One of your fellow-journalists honoured me with the label of a political painter immediately after August '80 because it was no longer forbidden.

Thirdly, my answer to the question of who I am is: I am a participant in, and a narrator of, reality. True to myself and my ideals, I seek to speak to people about people and things of immediate concern, about Poland, through my paintings. If there is pathos in what I say, see above, it is unintended and happens only when I speak about the essentials.

...I try to listen to the rhythm of life, weary daily routine, stiff formality, human complaints and human dreams, most often unfulfilled. I try to understand the mechanisms of irritation and wrath, vulgarity and stupidity. What I represent in my paintings already circulates in group consciousness and I only try to stop and "fix" all that, and turn hackneyed truths, social problems or background episodes into lasting human truths. Though my paintings may seem hideous, ugly, disturbing or painful, they are only paintings, they are painted reality, and people aware of it sometimes accept this portrait of reality.

...It is true that ten–fifteen years ago I bitterly and passionately attacked the effects of the social circumstances and the dubious historical heritage of Polish smugness and provincialism. It is true that after 1975 I made an effort to get to the causes of such attitudes, and even more than that. Today I look back with sentiment to the bitter year 1975 when, after the exhibition "Generation 30–40", I decided not to take part in any group exhibitions and competitions. I was determined to carry my "speaking pictures" round Poland all by myself.

...Today, rather than being satisfied with my loyalty to myself, with my choice, my right choice to be precise, rather than brimming with creative enthusiasm, I feel enervated, apathetic, prone to idle reflection. I dream of painting triumphant pageants of hypocrisy, boorishness and stupidity. Rather than praising national concord, I feel like painting despondency, empty talk and Poles being unable to communicate with one another. I feel even more tempted to paint lyrical landscapes because, to quote Witkacy, sometimes things get "too rotten, stinking, mendacious and disgusting".

...I have met real manual workers in my life because my father was one after the war, and I spent my childhood in Stradom, a peripheral, working-class district of Częstochowa. Just after obtaining my degree, I worked as a constructor for an industrial plant at Wełnowiec and, last but not least, I have lived in Silesia for twenty years now, and not in a villa with a swimming pool.

...Workers that I painted in the past and that I paint now are true to life because they are people. I do not paint a class ideal, a portrait of the working class, but live people. Some, like the expert plumber with rings on his fingers, are lazy shirkers, others, dull-brained and slothful, are almost the symbol of the legendary monsters of Polish building-plots that look like battle-fields. Have you never seen such workers? Finally, there are workers in *The Riders of the Apocalypse*. They are not three automatons but workmen of three generations rushing from one building site to another with a concrete mixer fixed to their buttocks. You have not mentioned my pictures painted after August 1980 where the working-class people are severe and angry. Let me repeat again that my painting has no class character. I do not paint workers on commission with guys, dressed up as if for a parade, posing to have their outfit portrayed. 113

I paint people whose ugliness and mediocrity, ridiculous traits and vices I find dear to my heart a beautiful.

...Besides the qualities mentioned above, like a literary and graphic quality, my paintings have been blamed for many other things like eclecticism, compilatory traits, primitivism and anti-intellectualism, but an absence of painterly qualities is the gravest charge. Taken together, all these charges do credit to my profession because of their number and emotional temperature. They are yet another proof that what I do is not only interesting to the public but also to the critics...

Are We That Ugly? Duda-Gracz Talks to Kazimierz Targosz, "Panorama", 1983, No. 11

...I didn't want to draw people to my picture, make them like it. I wanted it to repel them, frighten them away, and make them ask "why". Why is reality set in such hideous frames? What's going on? I realised that I should no longer deal with effects but had to try and show the causes... *The Polish Motif with Sausage* could be the answer to the questions I have been often asked: "Why do you attack workmen so violently?" Though there are pictures like this one of a workman who can be pacified neither with sausage nor with a decoration, but may well go on strike, no one has asked me questions about it. What is pointed out is my lampoons published in the "Szpilki" weekly in 1973. It is much more convenient to ask me about things which have passed through the sieve of the censorship, and turn a blind eye to what I am painting now. Even though the *Polish Motif with Sausage* features a workman, not an automaton. Suddenly, there is silence. No questions.

Q.: What about other paintings, *Polish Riding School IV, Polish Dances, Polish Dialogue?*

A.: Let's take the workman who is said to be the object of my attacks, and see what he looks like. Today it is certainly much easier to notice the lump of meat in the outfit of a member of the Establishment than the workman. He is too serious and so is the thrashing he may give. I have painted about ten *Polish Dialogues*. They are paintings about Poles being unable to communicate with one another. I treat many of them as preparatory studies for something bigger. I am thinking of a *Triumphant Pageant of Stupidity*. It is an eternal subject, especially stupidity in a national version, a mixture of hallucinations, stiltedness and historic conditions. It will have to be nightmarish, in the spirit of the dialogues, the inability to communicate on the most elementary matters... The reason for it may be that we cannot listen properly. We are not trying to understand one another. While listening, we shift our weight from one foot to the other, till the other guy stops talking and then we say what we want to say.

...I am trying to find a visual shape for expressing things like our stupidity, swank, parochial complexes and a lack of imagination. These are some of the heaviest plagues that afflict us. I am afraid that I may not be able to exhaust the subject and become stupid myself. *The Triumphant Pageant of Stupidity* and *The Triumphant Pageant of Boorishness* are the great subjects for which I still do not feel ready.

...To answer the question why people look at my paintings, one should read the visitors' books laid out at my exhibitions. The fever, the invectives and the words of encouragement have not improved my mood, but made me aware that there is some point in exerting myself, that these paintings have a public. It is no exaggeration, I can hardly underestimate a sentence like: "I feel embarrassed because I am a worker," or somebody's concern that the censorship might have overlooked something and I may get into trouble.

62. Jurassic Series, 1985

...I paint everything out of love. Even sinewy hands and wrinkles. When I paint two guys representing two different ideologies in a compulsory embrace, it is a little of a self-portrait because I am stranded somewhere between plus and minus, between black and white. This is how it should be interpreted. I am a little suspicious of myself, I haven't declared myself on any side, but my uncertainty results from my being true to myself, from the choice I have made. You can see it in the self-portrait *Ora et colabora* (1982). I merely try to record things because I perceive reality as so complex that despite my experience and sincere intents I merely present a faint echo of the day-by-day reality. It can't be caught up with and fully expressed.

...I don't know what art should do. There is no point in denuding reality. It is nude! I don't overestimate the social function of art, especially painting, because it has always been and will remain', elitist. I try to act against this evident principle myself, with some success with the public. I don't think that my generation will utter momentous truths anyway. Our blunders and errors will be the breeding ground for those who may say many wise things...

Iwona Rajewska, *Political Painter?*, ''Polityka'', 1983, No. 16

...Years ago, when I was a beginner, I was interested in the social lower depths, the stuffy and crammed peripheries, smugness, obscurantism, our national, almost historic ballast and flaws. As time went on, I realised I was forcing the wrong door and was in fact squaring accounts with effects rather than causes. I said to myself it was time I tried and recorded the sources of the present. That was in the mid-1970s. I decided to abstain from collective artistic life, group exhibitions and competitions to demonstrate my absence from the now absent group of eulogists of that reality. I painted the tormented ''builders'' of the second Tower of Babel, whom vodka and excessive success had made torpid, and riders of the Apocalypse, dances macabres and concerts for working-class people, Hamlets of the fields and pathetic lonely female idiots. Then came the years 1980 and 1981 with their nervous, hasty attempts at recording events day by day. The mood ranged from admiration and euphoria to anger, doubt, disappointment and bitterness. I painted *Polish Dances*, *Dialogues* and *Motifs*. And the *Polish Riding Schools*, almost a civil servant's pictorial report on Poland.

...I believe that vital social truths may be expressed in paintings, poems, films, theatre productions, cabaret songs. I believe that people, if they cannot do it themselves, expect someone to speak to them and for them about things that should not be left unsaid. There is a general demand for social truths, those expressed in the streets and in queues, and the great Polish truths. I simply try to remember these, treating my painting as a social duty. How people respond to it, is not my business.

...Rather than people, my criticism concerns situations, causes and effects that make people degenerate into swine, grow stupid, fall ill, drown and die. I need people to express myself on these situations and concepts. This is why I prefer mature models whom life has already formed. I walk past chicks' lovely phizs. Painting them would be pointless, devoid of expression, alien to my language...

Bogdan Brózda, *I Walk past Chicks' Lovely Phizs*, ''Walka Młodych'', 1983, No. 22

63. Jurassic Series, 1985

Curriculum Vitae

1941
Born in Częstochowa on 20 March.
1968
Graduated from the Academy of Fine Arts in Cracow (Department of Graphic Art and Design in Katowice).
1969
Admitted to the Polish Artists' Union.
1970
"Exhibition of Paintings and Etchings" (with graphic artist Tadeusz Siara), "Katowice" Gallery. Took part in the 3rd Polish Industrial Summer School in Bytom and the Polish Exhibition of Young Painting, Graphic Art and Sculpture in Sopot, Hel, Sztum, Gdynia, and Kwidzyń.
Awarded two drawn prizes in the Competition for a Monochromatic Drawing in Katowice, and an honourable mention in the 1st Polish Competition for a Painting in Łódź, and the Prize of the Board of Artistic Unions and Associations in Katowice for all artistic work.
Became full member of the Polish Artists' Union.
1971
One-man "Exhibition of Paintings and Drawings", Bureau for Art Exhibitions, Katowice; Gallery of the Polish Artists' Union, Cieszyn; Mały (Small) Theatre, Tychy; Gallery of the Polish Artists' Union, Sosnowiec.
One-man exhibition of drawings of the *Hospital* series, Provincial Hospital of the Ministry of the Interior, Katowice.
2nd prize in the Polish Drawing Competition "Nature and I...", Białowieża.
Collaborated as a set designer with the band "Silna Grupa pod Wezwaniem" (K. Grześkowiak, K. Litwin, J. Nieżychowski, A. Zakrzewski), Polish TV centres in Szczecin and Warsaw, and the Polish Film. Collaborated as a graphic designer with the Polskie Nagrania (Polish Recordings, until 1975).
1972
One-man "Exhibition of Paintings", Wielki (Grand) Theatre in Łódź; District House of Culture, Sieradz.
One-man exhibition of drawings of the *Hospital* series, Municipal Hospital, Głuchołazy.
"Permanent Display of Paintings by J. Duda-Gracz and J. Jańczak", Rajsek Gallery, Bosvil, Switzerland.
118   Took part in the 5th Polish Industrial Summer School in Zabrze; "Exhibition-Fair of Painting,

Graphic Art and Sculpture", "Katowice" Gallery; and the 1st Silesian Art Fair, Bureau for Art Exhibitions, Katowice.

Represented Poland at the exhibitions "Art from Poland", Svalov, Sweden; "Polish Art", Wert Galerie, Vienna, and "Polish Art", Tokuma Gallery, Tokyo.

Awarded the 1st prize in the competition "Region of Gliwice", Gliwice; 2nd prize and Silver Medal at the 10th Polish Painting Exhibition "Bielsko Autumn", Bielsko; 2nd Prize in the Competition "Woman", Katowice; 2nd prize in the 2nd Polish Competition for a Painting, Łódź, and the Prize of the Regional Board of the Polish Artists' Union at the regional exhibition "Katowice Salon '72", Katowice.

1973

One-man "Painting Exhibition", International Press and Book Club, Gliwice; one-man painting exhibition "Portraits" and "Polish Motifs", "Katowice" Gallery.

Took part in the 8th March Salon, Bureau for Art Exhibitions, Zakopane; 1st Triennale of Painting and Graphic Art "Our Time-Metaphor-Trends", Centre for the Popularisation of Art, Łódź, and the 13th Exhibition of Posters issued by the WAG Publishers, Show and Sports Hall, Katowice.

Took part in a summer school of the Hungarian Artists' Union in Tokaj, Hungary.

Represented Poland at the exhibition "Fantasy Painting", Skandinavska Enskilda Banken, Malmö, Sweden; and the exhibition "Painting, Weaving, Graphic Art and Sculpture", Kulturamt, Kiel, Germany.

Awarded the "Silver Pin '72" prize (for a socio-political cartoon), Warsaw and the 2nd prize at the Polish Festival "7th Opole Spring" (painting), Opole.

Collaborated as a graphic designer with the journals "Literatura", "Szpilki", "Filipinka", and "Poglądy" (until 1975).

1974

One-man shows "Portraits" and "Polish Motifs", Bureau for Art Exhibitions, Opole; Salon of the "Szpilki" weekly, Warsaw. Took part in the exhibitions: Polish Exhibition of Painting, Graphic Art and Sculpture "Interpretations", Bureau for Art Exhibitions, Szczecin; "Thirty Years of Painting in the People's Poland", Bureau for Art Exhibitions, Katowice; "Painters and Graphic Artists of the Province of Katowice. Panorama of Thirty Years", National Museum, Warsaw; 7th Festival of Contemporary Painting, Bureau for Art Exhibitions, Szczecin; "Documentation", Repassage Gallery, Warsaw; "Contemporary Young Polish Art", Sveagalleriet, Stockholm; "New 'Polonais' Movement", Espace Cardin, Paris; "Rassegna Internazionale Umoristia Marostica", Vicenza.

Awarded the 2nd prize at the Polish Exhibition "Contemporary Polish Socio-Politically Engaged Art", Łódź; 2nd prize at the 4th Drawing Triennale, Wrocław; "Golden Pin '73" (for a socio-political cartoon), Warsaw; 3rd prize at the Polish Exhibitions of Cartoons, Łódź; honourable mention in the competition for Warsaw's best poster of the month (September), Warsaw.

1975

One-man "Exhibition of Prints and Drawings", Bureau for Art Exhibitions, Wałbrzych; "Exhibition of Paintings" (with painter Henryk Waniek), Bureau for Art Exhibitions, Łódź; "Zapiecek" Gallery, Warsaw.

Took part in the exhibitions: "Warsaw's Best Poster '74", International Press and Book Club,

Warsaw; "Generation 30–40", Centre for the Popularisation of Art, Łódź; "Thirty Years of Art in the Region of Katowice", Bureau for Art Exhibitions, Katowice; "Exhibition of Paintings, Drawings and Miniatures" on the occasion of the 9th International Chopin Competition, National Philharmonic, Warsaw; "Poland '75" (International Fair 1975), Brussels; "Contemporary Polish Art", Nehrzweckhalle im Westfalenpark, Dortmund; "Thirty Years of Art in the Region of Katowice", Marktschlossen, Halle; House of Art, Ostrava; "Polish Art", Warleberger Hof Stadtmuseum, Kiel; Maison de Radio-France, Paris; "Vente Polonaise", Palais Galliera, Paris.

Awarded the C.K. Norwid Art Critics' Prize for the "Exhibition of Paintings" at the Salon of the "Szpilki" weekly, Warsaw; 1st prize at the 2nd Exhibition of Cartoons (for socio-political cartoons), Warsaw.

Collaborated as a graphic designer with the PIW publishers and Radio and Television Publishers.

In 1975, after the exhibition "Generation 30–40", J. Duda-Gracz gave up taking part in all forms of group artistic actions in favour of presenting his paintings at home on an exclusive basis. He hoped thus to establish the limits of his independence and responsibility for his own work. The display of his works at group exhibitions after 1975 was unauthorised.

1976

Works put on show in the framework of exhibitions: "Zapiecek Shows in 1972–6", Zapiecek Gallery, Warsaw; "50th Exhibition of Painting, Graphic Art and Drawing", Katowice Gallery; "Painting and Graphic Art from Ryszard Ratajczak's Collection", Kłodzko; "Contart '76", Lidzbark Warmiński; "Moderne Poolse Figuratieven", Eva Walińska Gallery, Arnhem.

Polish TV film *Duda-Gracz* (script: Wisława Karłowska, Janina Gierak; photography director: Paweł Minkiewicz), made in 1975, awarded the "Golden Pegasus" Grand Prix, the prize of the Polish Artists' Union, the prize of the A. Kenar School in Zakopane and the prize of the public at the 9th Polish Survey of Art Films, Zakopane, 1976.

Scholarship awarded by the Fund for the Development of the Fine Arts at the Ministry of Culture and Art.

Appointed a lecturer of painting and drawing at the Katowice branch of the Academy of Fine Arts in Cracow.

1977

Works put on show in the framework of exhibitions:

"From the Collection of the Warsaw Bureau for Art Exhibitions", MDM Gallery, Warsaw; Prize-winners of the C.K. Norwid Prize, Artist's House, Warsaw; "Contart '77", Olsztyn.

1978

One-man "Exhibition of Paintings", Central Bureau for Art Exhibitions. "Kordegarda" Gallery, Warsaw .

Took part in the exhibitions: "Folk Culture – National Culture", Central Bureau for Art Exhibitions, "Zachęta Gallery, Warsaw; "Man's Thruth – Artist's Thruth", Bureau for Art Exhibitions, "Avant-garde" Gallery, Wrocław.

1979

One-man "Exhibition of Paintings", Bureau for Art Exhibitions – Bałucka Gallery, Łódź; Regional Museum, Toruń; Bureau for Art Exhibitions "Arsenal", Poznań; Bureau for Art Exhibitions, Olsztyn; Bureau for Art Exhibitions, Wałbrzych; Bureau for Art Exhibitions,

64. Jurassic Series, 1985

Kłodzko; Bureau for Art Exhibitions, Opole; Gallery of the Society of the Friends of Sopot, Sopot; Bureau for Art Exhibitions, Słupsk; Bureau for Art Exhibitions, Lublin; Bureau for Art Exhibitions, Koszalin; Bureau for Art Exhibitions, Katowice; Bureau for Art Exhibitions "Avant-garde" Gallery, Wrocław; Workers' "Hutmen" Gallery, Wrocław.

Represented at the exhibition "The Poles' Own Portrait", National Museum, Cracow.

On the 35th anniversary of the People's Poland awarded the Prime Minister's second-class prize "For outstanding achievements as a painter".

1980

One-man "Exhibition of Paintings", Bureau for Art Exhibitions, Bydgoszcz; Bureau for Art Exhibitions, Tarnów; Bureau for Art Exhibitions, Zakopane; Pryzmat Gallery, Cracow; "Oficyna" Gallery in the Regional Museum, Gorzów Wielkopolski; Bureau for Art Exhibitions, Jelenia Góra.

Works presented in the framework of exhibitions: "Thirty-five Years of Painting in the People's Poland", Central Bureau for Art Exhibitions, "Zachęta" Gallery, Warsaw; "In the Sphere of Metaphor Paintings", Polish Culture Institute, London.

Collaborated as a stage designer with the S. Wyspiański Silesian Theatre in Katowice, and as a graphic designer with the Współczesny (Contemporary) Theatre in Szczecin.

1981

One-man "Exhibition of Paintings from 1976–81", Bureau for Art Exhibitions, Szczecin; Bureau for Art Exhibitions, Kielce. Works presented in the framework of exhibitions "Woman's Image" paintings, graphic art and drawing from W. Siemion's Rural Gallery, Bureau for Art Exhibitions, Piotrków Trybunalski; "Polish Painting 1944–79" (from the collection of the Regional Museum in Bydgoszcz), Central Bureau for Art Exhibitions "Zachęta" Gallery, Warsaw; "Polnische Metaphorische Malerei", Centre of Information and Polish Culture, Berlin.

Collaborated as a graphic designer with the Literary Publishers and the Polish Music Publishers in Cracow.

Appointed assistant professor at the Department of Painting of the Academy of Fine Arts in Cracow.

1982

Took part in the Jasna Góra Summer School in Częstochowa. Resumed participation in group forms of artistic action. Gave up teaching at the Katowice branch of the Academy of Fine Arts in Cracow.

1983

One-man show "Polish Paintings", Bureau for Arts Exhibitions, Łódź; the first public presentation of the painting *Exodus* during conductor Karol Stryja's anniversary concert (Berlioz, Kilar) with the Great Symphony Orchestra of the Polish Radio and Television WOSPRiT, Cultural Centre, Katowice.

Took part in the exhibition "Presentation of Works Donated to and Purchased for the National Museum", National Museum, Warsaw. Took part in the Polish Plein Airt "9th Jurassic Autumn", Częstochowa.

Contributed to the "Panorama" weekly as a columnist, Katowice.

1984

The first public presentation of the painting *Krzesany* during the conductor Witold Rowicki's anniversary concert ("Tatra Morning", Szymanowski, Kilar), WOSPRiT Orchestra, Cutural Centre, Katowice.

One-man "Exhibition of paintings from 1968–84", Bureau for Art Exhibitions, Katowice.

Took part in the exhibitions: "20th-century Polish Painting", National Museum, Cracow; "Polish Portrait Painting 1944–84", Central Bureau for Art Exhibitions, "Zachęta" Gallery, Warsaw; International Art Fair of Socialist Countries, Poznań.

Took part in the 10th Plein Air "Jurassic Autumn", Częstochowa.

Represented at the exhibitions "Polish Art during the Forty Years of the People's Poland", Manège, Moscow; "Fantasy and Metaphor in Painting", Polish Institute, Paris; 41st International Biennale of Art, Polish Pavilion, Venice; "Painting of the Katowice Region of the Polish Union of Painters and Graphic Artists", Miskolc, Budapest.

Collaborated as a stage designer with the Stary Theatre in Cracow (the Small Stage) on Andrzej Dziuk's production of the play *Gra o każdym* (*Play on Everybody*).

Became founder-member of the Union of Polish Painters and Graphic Artists and member of its provisional board. The Minister of Culture and Art appointed J. Duda-Gracz member of the Programme Committee of the Contemporary Art Centre in Warsaw.

1985

One-man "Exhibition of Paintings from 1968–84", Central Bureau for Art Exhibitions "Zachęta" Gallery, Warsaw; one-man "Exhibition of Jurassic Paintings", Gallery '72, Museum of Chełm; "Malereiaustellung – Jerzy Duda-Gracz – 'Jurabilder'", Polnisches Informations und Kulturzentrium Berlin; Leipzig.

Took part in the exhibitions: "Jurassic Autumn '84", post-plein-air show, Bureau for Art Exhibitions, Częstochowa; Gallery of the Forty Years ("Przekrój" 1945–85 – forty paintings of the Forty Years), National Museum, Cracow; "Forty Years of the Work of the Artists of the Katowice Province", Bureau for Art Exhibitions, Katowice; 11th Survey of Painters of Socalist Countries, Bureau for Art Exhibitions, Szczecin; "Forty Victorious Years" Manège, Moscow; "International Exhibition of East Europan Art", Cultural Centrum, Rotterdam; "Woman as Seen by Some Polish Artists", 102 Gallery, Rome; "Works Purchased by, Donated to, and Deposited with the Silesian Museum in Katowice", Bureau for Art Exhibitions, Katowice; "Exhibition from the collection of the Central Bureau for Art Exhibitions", "Zachęta" Gallery, Warsaw; "Contemporary Polish Portrait Painting", Museumspavillon des Mirabell-Gartens, Salzburg; "3rd Polish Painting Plein Airt – Grunwald '85", Bureau for Art Exhibitions, Olsztyn; 2nd International Art Fair of Socialist Countries "Interart '85", Poznań; "Exhibition on the 50th Anniversary of the 'Szpilki' Weekly", Warsaw; "Contemporary Polish Protraiture", Modern Art Centre, St Poelten Museum, Austria; "Woman in Art", Institute of Polish Culture, Prague, Stockholm; "Polish Painting", Beijing.

Director of the Museum of Upper Silesia in Bytom made J. Duda-Gracz the offer of placing a gallery at his exclusive disposal. By a deed of gift made on 5 March 1985, J. Duda-Gracz donated thirty paintings, seven drawings and prints and current documentation of his work to the Town of Bytom and promised to complement the donation with at least two works every year in future.

On 25 March, the People's Town Council in Bytom passed resolution No. VI/45/85 concerning the institution of "Duda-Gracz's Gallery" based in the Museum of Upper Silesia in Bytom.

123

The Gallery was inaugurated on 17 December at a ceremony preceded by a concert highlighting Bogna Sokorska.

Józef Gębski made a film about Jerzy Duda-Gracz's self-portrait for the WFD (Documentary Film Producers).

President of the City of Katowice awarded the W. Roździeński prize for "artistic work and social activity" to J. Duda-Gracz.

The Voivode of Katowice awarded the Provincial Prize for "his entire artistic work and outstanding achievements as a painter" to J. Duda-Gracz.

The Minister of Culture and Art awarded J. Duda-Gracz a first-class prize for "artistic work in 1985" (and especially the series of painting on contemporary subjects presented at the "Zachęta" Gallery in Warsaw in 1985).

1986

One-man shows:"Paintings by Jerzy Duda-Gracz", Institute of Polish Culture, London; "Jerzy Duda-Gracz. Dutch Paintings", Society of the Friends of Fine Arts, Warsaw;"Portraits by Jerzy Duda-Gracz", Bureau for Art Exhibitions, Radom;"Duda-Gracz. Dutch Paintings", Bureau for Art Exhibitions, Gdańsk;"Duda-Gracz. Exhibition of Jurassic Paintings", Bureau for Art Exhibitions, Łódź;"Travelling Far and Near", painting exhibition. Lengyel Tájékcztató és Kulturális Központ, Budapest; Úttörö Ifjúsági és Müvelödési Központ, Budapest,"Jerzy Duda-Gracz. Exhibition of Jurassic Paintings", Władysław Hasior Gallery, Zakopane, Bureau for Art Exhibitions, Poznań ("Arsenal"), Bureau for Art Exhibitions, Białystok;"Duda-Gracz. Peinture, Tableaux Jurassiques", Polish Institute, Paris;"Jerzy Duda-Gracz. Malereiausstellung 'Jurabilder' ("Polnische Tagen"), Merzig, Federal Republic of Germany.

Took part in the exhibitions:"Human Life. The Fate of the Earth", Central Bureau for Art Exhibitions,"Zachęta" Gallery, Warsaw;"Polish Painting", Sian, Chengtu (People's China). Exhibition of works by guests invited to a session of the Parliamentary Cultural Committee, Seym building, Warsaw;"11th Jurassic Autumn '85", post-plein-air exhibition, Bureau for Art Exhibitions, Częstochowa; "Brücke Zwischen Ost und West", Rheinmuseum, Emmerich, Federal Republic of Germany;"1st Polish Exhibition of Painting and Graphic Art by members of the Union of Polish Painters and Graphic Artists", Central Bureau for Art Exhibitions, "Zachęta" Gallery, Warsaw;"Contemporary Polish Art","De Ossekop" Gallery, Utrecht;"1st Biennale of Painting and Graphic Art of the Katowice Region of the Union of Polish Painters and Graphic Artists", Bureau for Art Exhibitions, Katowice;"Sztuka" Collection, Gallery '85, Gdańsk;"Contemporary Polish Painting", Galerie Am Weidendamm, Berlin; Exhibition of the Katowice Region of the Union of Polish Painters and Graphic Artists, Gdańsk, Kielce, Bielsko-Biała, Karlovy Vary;"Sztuka" Collection,"El" Gallery, Elbląg, Central Bureau for Art Exhibitions"Kordegarda" Gallery, Warsaw, Bureau for Art Exhibitions, Olsztyn,"Stara Kordegarda" Gallery, Warsaw; 3rd International Art Fair of Socialist Countries"Interart '86", Poznań; "Realistic Trends in Contemporary Polish Painting", Bureau for Art Exhibitions, Bydgoszcz; "Woman in Contemporary Polish Painting", National Philharmonic, Warsaw; 20 Internationaler Kunstmarkt, Cologne;"Painting and Graphic Art of Katowice Artists; Institute of Information and Polish Culture, Prague. Jerzy Duda-Gracz joined the All-Polish Peace Committee and the National Council of Culture.

An album presenting Jerzy Duda-Gracz's oeuvre won the title of the Book of the Month and the artist received an"Honourable Diploma of the Warsaw Literary Première".

On 20 March 1986, the Lejderman family planted seven trees for J. Duda-Gracz in Yatir, Israel. The Society of the Lovers of Bytom awarded J. Duda-Gracz the Individual Prize of the Year. The Voivode of Częstochowa awarded Jerzy Duda-Gracz a prize for his set of work at the "1st Biennale of Painting and Graphic Art of the Katowice Region of the Union of Polish Painters and Graphic Artists".

1987

One-man shows: "Jurassic Paintings. Painting of Jerzy Duda-Gracz", Institute of Polish Culture, Vienna; "Duda-Gracz. Jurassic Paintings. Painting", Institute of Polish Culture, Stockholm; "Jerzy Duda-Gracz. Painting (1968–1986)", Central House of the Artist, Moscow.

Took part in the exhibitions: "Portrait", Museum of Chorzów; "Workers in Art, Photography and Documents", Gallery of the Silesian Library, Katowice: "Contemporary Polish Art 1945–87", National Museum, Warsaw; "Eros in Caricatures", Caricature Museum, Warsaw; 4th Triennale "Contemporary Portraiture Survey", Bureau for Art Exhibitions, Cracow; "Portraits in Polish Posters", Havana; "Contemporary Painting of the Region of Katowice", Art Gallery, Ostrava; "Polnische Karikaturisten der Gegenwart", Westfälisches Landesmuseum, Münster, Wilhelm Busch Museum, Hannover; "Contemporary Visual Arts in Poland", Manège, Moscow; "Exhibition of Polish Art" (B. Biegas, J. Duda-Gracz, A. Krajewski, S. Knapp), Saville Club, London; "Contemporary Portraits from Poland", Rhyl Library Museum and Art Centre, Rhyl, Great Britain; "21st International Art Fair", Cologne; 4th International Art Fair of Socialist Countries "Interart '87", Poznań; "Sztuka" Collection, Academy of Fine Arts, Budapest, Institute of Polish Culture, Stockholm.

Took part in the 11th Polish Plein Air organised in the village of Kamion by the Bureau for Art Exhibitions in Sieradz. The Board of the Society of the Friends of Fine Arts in Warsaw awarded J. Duda-Gracz a diploma and medal issued on the Society's 25th anniversary for the "Art Event of the Year 1986" for his exhibition of "Dutch Paintings" held at the Society's "Pałacyk" Gallery in Warsaw.

1988

One-man shows: "Jerzy Duda-Gracz. Painting", 102 Gallery, Rome; "Ausstellung Jerzy Duda-Gracz (Die Polnische Kulturtage), Fürth, Federal Republic of Germany; "Jerzy Duda-Gracz. Painting", Gallery of the BAWAG Foundation, Vienna; "Jerzy Duda-Gracz. Painting", Centre of Information and Polish Culture, Sofia; "Jerzy Duda-Gracz. Paintings", Lorentzon Gallery, Stockholm; "Jerzy Duda-Gracz. Painting", Mirbach Palace, Bratislava.

Took part in the exhibitions: The Fruit of the 11th Plein Air "Somewhere in the Middle of Poland – Kamion '87", Bureau for Art Exhibitions, Sieradz; "2nd Biennale of Painting and Graphic Art of the Katowice Region of the Union of Polish Painters and Graphic Artists", Bureau for Art Exhibitions, Katowice; "Contemporary Polish Painting" (from the collection of the Central Office for Art Exhibitions), Vitebsk; "Contemporary Polish Painting", Lvov Gallery of Paintings, Church of the Nuns of the Order of St. Clare, Lvov; "Contemporary Polish Art", Delhi, Madras; "Contemporary Polish Drawing", Polish Institute, Paris.

Took part in the 12th Polish Plein Air in the village of Kamion organised by the Bureau for Art Exhibitions in Sieradz. The Department of Culture and Art of the Provincial Office in Sieradz awarded J. Duda-Gracz a prize for his set of works presented at the post-plein-air exhibition "Somewhere in the Middle of Poland – Kamion '87".

Collaborated as a stage designer with the Silesian Opera House in Bytom on the production of G. Bizet's *Carmen* conducted by J. Salwarowski, directed by M. Fołtyn and choreographed by K. Gruszkówna.

The Minister of Foreign Affairs awarded J. Duda-Gracz a diploma of merit for his outstanding achievements in the popularisation of Polish culture abroad.

The Polish Radio in Katowice awarded J. Duda-Gracz the J. Ligoń prize.

Jerzy Duda-Gracz was invited to join the Foundation of Polish Culture and elected member of the Foundation Board.

The editors of the "Przekrój" weekly organised an auction of three paintings by J. Duda-Gracz at the Bureau for Art Exhibitions. The proceeds were given to the Foundation of Polish Culture.

Zbigniew Raplewski made a documentary film entitled *Jerzy Duda-Gracz's Inspirations* for the Polish Television.

1989

One-man shows: "Mostra del Pittore Jerzy Duda-Gracz", Palazzo Pinucci, Florence; "Jerzy Duda-Gracz. Exhibition of Painting", House of Detention, Gliwice; "Paintings by Jerzy Duda-Gracz", Institute of Polish Culture, London; "Jerzy Duda-Gracz's Painting", Bureau for Art Exhibitions, Sieradz; "U Jaksy" Gallery, Bureau for Art Exhibitions, Miechów, Bureau for Art Exhibitions, Zamość; "Jerzy Duda-Gracz Gemälde – Zyklus 'Jurabilder'", Galerie Dorota Kabiesz, Düsseldorf.

Took part in the exhibitions: "Motif of the Road in Polish Painting", Regional Museum, Rzeszów; Auction of Works of Art "Hevelius '89", Heweliusz Hotel, Gdańsk; Fruit of the 12th Sieradz Plein-Air "Somewhere in the Middle of Poland – Kamion '89", Bureau for Art Exhibitions, Sieradz; "30 Years of the Society of the Friends of Fine Arts in Warsaw", "Stara Kordegarda" Gallery, Warsaw; "Contemporary Polish Painting", Centre of Information and Polish Culture, Berlin; "Silesian Ex-libris", Gallery of the Silesian Library, Katowice; "Exhibition of Purchased and Donated Works", Museum of Warmia and Mazury, Olsztyn.

Took part in the 13th Polish Plein Art in the village of Kamion organised by the Bureau for Art Exhibitions in Sieradz. Founded a money-box for the benefit of the Foundation of Polish Culture at his "Autorska (D'Auteur) Gallery" in Bytom.

J. Duda-Gracz became the "honorary godfather" of the new exhibition salon of the Bureau for Art Exhibitions in Sieradz.

The Cracow daily "Gazeta Krakowska" awarded J. Duda-Gracz its traditional medal "For Wisdom and Good Work".

The Warsaw daily "Trybuna Ludu" awarded J. Duda-Gracz its first-class Individual Prize for outstanding achievements in painting and for the popularisation of Polish Art.

The Department of Culture and Art of the Provincial Office in Sieradz awarded J. Duda-Gracz a prize for his set of works presented at the post-plein-air exhibition "Somewhere in the Middle of Poland – Kamion '88".

Bishop of Katowice Damian Zimoń consecrated the chapel of the Nuns of the Order of Our Lady, designed by J. Duda-Gracz.

1990

One-man shows: "Jerzy Duda-Gracz's Paintings", Museum of the Town of Pabianice; "Jerzy

Duda-Gracz's Paintings'', Lorentzon Gallery, Stockholm;''Jerzy Duda-Gracz's Painting'',
Gallery 58, Chicago;''Jerzy Duda-Gracz's Painting'', Delhi.
Took part in the exhibitions:''Exhibition of Painting and Graphic Art. Union of Polish Painters
and Graphic Artists'',''Dworcowa'' Gallery, Katowice; 14th Polish Plein Air, Bureau for Art
Exhibitions, Sieradz.
The Department of Culture and Art of the Provincial Office in Sieradz awarded J. Duda-Gracz
a prize for his set of works presented at the post-plein-air exhibition''Somewhere in the
Middle of Poland — Kamion '89''.

Bibliography

1. K. Grześkowiak *Wystawa obrazów i akwafort (Exhibition of Paintings and Etchings)*, catalogue introduction, Katowice, 1970
2. B. Surówka *Obrazy i akwaforty (Paintings and Etchings)*"Dziennik Zachodni", 311, 1970
3. K. Grześkowiak *Wystawa obrazów i rysunków (Exhibition of Paintings and Drawings)*, catalogue introduction, Katowice, 1971
4. M. Wroński *Rozmowa z Jerzym Dudą-Graczem (Talking to Jerzy Duda-Gracz)*"Poglądy", 11, 1971
5. K. Grześkowiak *Sam to powiem i powiem więcej (I'll Say It Myself, and I'll Say More)*"Polityka", 21, 1971
6. A. Osęka *Wdzięk prowincjonalny (Provincial Charm)* "Polska" 8, 1971 (Poland, Oct, 1971)
7. K. Grześkowiak *Wystawa obrazów (Exhibition of Paintings,* catalogue introduction), Teatr Wielki (Grand Theatre), Łódź, 1972
8. A. Ligocki *Plastyka i fotografia artystyczna (Visual Arts and Art Photography)*"Almanach Kulturalny", Katowice, 1972
9. S. Piskor *Bielska jesień '72 (Autumn in Bielsko '72)*"Dziennik Zachodni", 331, 1972
10. W. Orfin *Czym sztuka polska bogata... (The Boast of Polish Art...)*"Trybuna Robotnicza", Jan, 1973
11. M. Podolska *Wizytówka (Visiting Card)*"Trybuna Robotnicza", 21 Jan, 1973
12. S. Piskor *Zmistyfikowana świadomość (Consciousness Mystified)*"Dziennik Zachodni", 27 Jan, 1973
13. J. Duda-Gracz *O obrazie, czyli jak do tego doszło (On the Picture of How It Has Come to That)*, "Poglądy", 7, 1973
14. J. Jurczyk *Nasz czas – metafora – tendencje (Our Time – Metaphor – Trends)*"Przekrój", 1474, 1973
15. J. Fensette *Dziesięcioro przesądów na Opolską Wiosnę (Ten Superstitions for the Opole Spring)* "Opole", 7, 1973
16. H. Anders *Nasz czas – metafora – tendencje (Our Time – Metaphor – Trends)*"Przegląd Artystyczny", 6, 1973
17. A. Ligocki *Portrety i motywy polskie (Portraits and Polish Motifs)*, catalogue introduction, Katowice Gallery, 1974
18. J. Kofta, J. Kulmowa, R.M. Groński *Portrety i motywy polskie (Portraits and Polish Motifs)*, catalogue introduction, Salon of the"Szpilki" weekly, Warsaw, 1974
19. S. Piskor *Polski pop-art J. Dudy-Gracza (J. Duda-Gracz's Polish Pop Art)*"Dziennik Zachodni", 15, 1974
20. (Buss) *Jerzy Duda-Gracz*"ITD", 5, 1974
21. Z.J. *Dziewczyna Jerzego Dudy-Gracza (Jerzy Duda-Gracz's Girl)*"Filipinka", 3, 1974
22. J. Jurczyk *Interpretacje (Interpretations)*"Poezja", 3, 1974
23. J. and A. Skoczylas *Pierwsza aukcja (The First Auction)*"Kultura", 15, 1974
24. M. Podolska *Jerzy Duda-Gracz* "Poglądy", 8, 1974

25. L. Wieluński *Wieczory w 'Espace Cardin'* (*Evenings at the 'Espace Cardin'*)"Perspektywy", 19, 1974

26. K. Zienkiewicz *Ilustrowanie wad i przywar* (*Illustrating Vices and Flaws*)"Trybuna Opolska", 146, 1974

27. J. Jurczyk *Szczecińskie interpretacje* (*Szczecin Interpretations*)"Sztuka", 3, 1974

28. A. Skoczylas *Aukcja sztuki polskiej w Paryżu* (*Auction of Polish Art in Paris*)"Sztuka", 3, 1974

29. F. Netz *Katowicki Salon Plastyki* (*Art Salon in Katowice*)"Panorama", 23, 1974

30. S. Bojko *W pracowniach młodych grafików* (*In the Studios of Young Graphic Artists*)"Projekt", 4, 1974

31. Beta *Duda-Gracz, Studio i Koszalin* (*Duda-Gracz, Studio and Koszalin*)"Życie Literackie", 38, 1974

32. (A) *Mówi Duda-Gracz, czyli śmieszne obrazki* (*Duda-Gracz Speaking or Funny Pictures*)"Kulisy", 37, 1974

33. *M. Czerwiński obejrzał obrazy J. Dudy-Gracza* (*M. Czerwiński Has Seen J. Duda-Gracz's Paintings*)"Szpilki", 40, 1974

34. K. Zienkiewicz *Stare sztychy i polskie motywy* (*Old Prints and Polish Motifs*)"Opole", 7, 1974

35. Z. J. *Jerzy Duda-Gracz* "Filipinka", 20, 1974

36. W. Krauze *Plastycy z Katowic w Muzeum Narodowym* (*Katowice Artists in the National Museum*) "Życie Warszawy", 3–4 Nov, 1974

37. E.B. *Barwy ziemi i ludzi. 30 lat malarstwa w PRL* (*Colours of Earth and People. 30 Years of Painting in the People's Poland*)"Panorama", 44, 1974

38. (NER) *Sztuka Śląska i Zagłębia w Warszawie* (*The Art of Silesia and the Coal Basin in Warsaw*) "Trybuna Ludu", 311, 1974

39. S. Piskor *Jerzy Duda-Gracz* "Student", 30 Oct, 1974

40. H. Waniek *Wystawa obrazów – Duda-Gracz, Waniek* (*Exhibition of Paintings. Duda-Gracz, Waniek*), catalogue introduction, Bureau for Art Exhibitions, Łódź. 1975; "Zapiecek" Gallery, Warsaw

41. (jah) *Wie co i jak* (*Know-what, know-how*)"Trybuna Wałbrzyska", 2, 1975

42. (ega) *Laureaci Nagrody Norwida* (*Winners of the Norwid Prize*)"Trybuna Ludu", 34, 1975

43. G. Romanowski *Słowo do „Pokolenia 30–40"* (*Gloss on "Generation 30–40"*)"Głos Robotniczy", 1975

44. A. Osęka *Prostaczek przewrotny* (*A Perverse Simpleton*) "Polska" 2, 1975 ("Poland" Feb., 1975)

45. W. Guyski *Na motywach prowincjonalnych* (*On Provincial Motifs*)"Projekt", 1, 1975

46. H. Jałowiecka *Malarstwo Jerzego Dudy-Gracza* (*Painting of Jerzy Duda-Gracz*)"Dziennik Zachodni", 12–13 April, 1975

47. G. Romanowski *Malarstwo z daleka, malarstwo z bliska* (*Painting from Far, Painting from Near*) "Głos Robotniczy", 15 May, 1975

48. M. Jagoszewski *Człowiek i architektura* (*Man and Architecture*)"Dziennik Łódzki", 102, 1975

49. *Nagroda im. C.K. Norwida* (*The C.K. Norwid Award*)"Projekt", 3, 1975

50. B. Kowalska *Kronika* (*Chronicle*)"Sztuka", 3, 1975

51. S. Piskor *Jerzy Duda-Gracz* "Poglądy", 12, 1975

52. A. Lechicka *Na wystawie obrazów J. Dudy-Gracza i H. Wańka* (*At the Exhibition of Paintings by J. Duda-Gracz and H. Waniek*)"Szpilki", 36, 1975

53. W. Skrodzki *Spółka z pełną odpowiedzialnością* (*Company with Full Liability*)"Literatura", 4 Sept, 1975

54. W. Stradomski *Duda-Grcz i inni* (*Duda-Gracz and Others*)"Radio and TV", 1975

55. M. Gutowski *Złe i dobre samopoczucie* (*Bad and Good Frame of Mind*)"Kultura", 20, 1976

56. Ł. Heyman *Jerzy Duda-Gracz* "Nowy Wyraz", 2, 1976

57. M. Podolska *Cierpko i lirycznie* (*In a Bitter and Lyrical Vein*)"Panorama", 20, 1976

58. M. Sienkiewicz *Sztuka filmowania sztuki* (*The Art of Filming Art*)"Przekrój", 1622, 1976

59. S. Piskor *Sztuka, Obraz, Piękno – nie umarły*. Rozmowa z J. Dudą-Graczem (*Art, Paintings, Beauty Have not Died.* Talking to J. Duda-Gracz)"Poglądy", 12, 1976

60. (jot) *Wybitny malarz przygotowuje nową wystawę* (*Outstanding Painter Prepares a New Exhibition*)"Wieczór", 3–5 Sept, 1976

61. A. Skoczylas *Laureaci Nagrody Krytyki im. C.K. Norwida* (*Winners of the C.K. Norwid Critics' Award*), catalogue introduction. Artist's House, Warsaw 1977

62. (MAP) *10 lat Nagrody im. Norwida. Znaki zapytania* (10 Years of the Norwid Award. Question Marks)"Trybuna Ludu", 68, 1977

63. A. Osęka *Najlepsi z najlepszych* (*The Very Best*)"Kultura", 9, 1977

64. M. Gutowski *Wybory właściwe* (*The Right Choice*)"Kultura", 14, 1977

65. B. Nowicka „*Contart '77*'"Sztandar Młodych", 128, 1977

66. H. Panas *Blaski i cienie awangardy* (*Splendours and Miseries of Avant-garde*)"Gazeta Olsztyńska", 125, 1977

67. H. Panas *Udany „Contart '77*" (*Successful* "*Contart '77*")"Gazeta Olsztyńska", 130, 1977

68. A. Skoczylas *Nagroda Krytyki im. C.K. Norwida* (*The C.K. Norwid Critics' Prize*)"Sztuka", 2, 1977

69. A. Kępińska *Nowe modele konfiguracji w latach 60. i ich kontynuacje* (*New Configuration Models in the 1960s and their Continuation*)"Sztuka", 3, 1977

70. B. Majewska *Krytycy i twórcy* (*Critics and Artists*)"Projekt", 3, 1977

71. S. Wyszyńska *Ci trzej z Katowic* (*The Trio of Katowice*)"Razem", 27, 1977

72. G. Hołub *Piosenki z pracowni* (*Songs from a Studio*)"Nowa Wieś", 29, 1977

73. B.K. "*Contart '77*'"Sztuka", 4, 1977

74. H. Panas *Komu Dudę-Gracza komu Kantora* (*Who Wants Duda-Gracz, who Wants Kantor*) "Kontrasty", 8, 1977

75. A. Iskierko *Piosenki z pracowni* (*Songs from a Studio*)"Ekran", 43, 1977

76. (j) *Sukcesy wybitnego artysty* (*Outstanding Artist's Success*)"Wieczór", 240, 1977

77. A. Osęka *Satyra jest rzeczą poważną* (*Satire is a Serious Thing*) "Szpilki", 46, 1977

78. W. Skrodzki *Wystawa obrazów* (*Exhibition of Paintings*), catalogue introduction,"Kordegarda" Gallery, Warsaw, 1978

79. (gal) *Aukcja* (*Auction*)"Kurier Lubelski", 93, 1978

80. *Jerzy Duda-Gracz* "ITD", 15, 1978

81. J.M. *Jerzy Duda-Gracz*"Poezja", 5, 1978

82. B. Kowalska *O kierunkach w sztuce – inaczej* (*On Trends in Art* – Differently)"Odra", 6, 1978

83. A. Kiszkis *Jacy jesteśmy? Odpowiadają plastycy z 13 krajów* (*What Are We Like? Artists from Thirteen Countries Speak*)"Dziennik Ludowy", 187, 1978

84. S. Piskor *W odpowiedzi polemistom* (*Answering the Adversaries*)"Poglądy", 18, 1978

85. E. Wybraniec *Zaledwie prymus czy już artysta?* (*Merely a Top Boy or an Artist?*)"Trybuna Robotnicza", 23–24 Oct, 1978

86. T. Nyczek *Przez okulary Sławomira Mrożka* (*Through Sławomir Mrożek's Glasses*)"Miesięcznik Literacki", 11, 1978

87. W. Budzyński *Obraz jaki jest – każdy widzi* (*A Picture as It Is – Everybody Sees*)"Sztandar Młodych", 296, 1978

88. (J. R-K) *Wystawa Dudy-Gracza* (*Duda-Gracz's Exhibition*)"Dziennik Ludowy", 288, 1978

89. K. Prynda *Kolejny sukces J. Dudy-Gracza* (*J. Duda-Gracz's Another Success*)"Wieczór", 285, 1978

90. M. Sztokfisz *Kto nie lubi Dudy-Gracza* (*Who Doesn't Like Duda-Gracz*)"Sztandar Młodych", 297, 1978

91. *Spacerkiem po warszawskich wystawach* (*Walking through Warsaw Exhibitions*)"Express Wieczorny", 284, 1978

92. M. Jaworski *Między satyrą i poezją* (*Between Satire and Poetry*)"Trybuna Ludu", 305, 1978

93. A. Skoczylas *O sztuce faktu* (*On Non-fiction Art*)"Sztuka", 6, 1978

94. W. Skrodzki *Wystawa obrazów* (*Exhibition of Paintings*), catalogue introduction, BWA Gallery in Łódź, 1979; BWA Gallery in Opole, 1979; BWA Gallery in Katowice, 1979

95. B. Kowalska *Wystawa obrazów* (*Exhibition of Paintings*), catalogue introduction, BWA Gallery "Arsenał" in Poznań, 1979

96. K.T. Toeplitz *Wystawa obrazów* (*Exhibition of Paintings*), catalogue introduction, Regional Museum in Toruń, 1979; BWA Gallery in Olsztyn, 1979; TSP Gallery in Sopot, 1979

97. Z. Mentzel *Duda-Gracz w"Kordegardzie"* (*Duda-Gracz at the"Kordegarda"*)"Polityka", 1, 1979

98. *Malarstwo Jerzego Dudy-Gracza* (*Jerzy Duda-Gracz's Painting*)"Gazeta Olsztyńska", 14, 1979

99. *Malarstwo Jerzego Dudy-Gracza* (*Jerzy Duda-Gracz's Painting*)"Gazeta Współczesna", 14, 1979

100. *Malarstwo Jerzego Dudy-Gracza* (*Jerzy Duda-Gracz's Painting*)"Gazeta Pomorska", 20, 1979

101. (grom) *Duda-Gracz w Galerii Bałuckiej* (*Duda-Gracz at the Bałucka Gallery*)"Głos Robotniczy", 8, 1979

102. *Duda-Gracz w "Kordegardzie"* (*Duda-Gracz at the"Kordegarda" Gallery*)"Poglądy", 4, 1979

103. M. Hniedziewicz *Pastisz i publicystyka* (*Pastiche and Journalism*)"Kultura", 5, 1979

104. A. Majer *Komiks objazdowy* (*Touring Comic Strip*)"Odgłosy", 5, 1979

105. A. Grun *Duda-Gracz, czyli"szczęśliwość w głupocie"* (*Duda-Gracz or"Happiness in Stupidity"*) "Dziennik Popularny", 29, 1979

106. K. Mroziewicz *Pamiątka z pracowni* (*Souvenir from a Studio*)"ITD", 6, 1979

107. (ks) *Toruńska wystawa obrazów Dudy-Gracza* (*Toruń Exhibition of Duda-Gracz's Paintings*) "Gazeta Pomorska", 3, 1979

108. A. Męczyńska, *Postaram się poprawić* (*I'll Try to Improve*)"Nowości", 43, 1979

109. *Kto nie lubi Dudy-Gracza* (*Who Doesn't Like Duda-Gracz*) "Profile", 3, 1979

110. T. Marciniak *Fikcja i prawda* (*Fiction and Truth*) "Nowości", 49, 1979

111. B. Lubosz *Katowiczanin w Warszawie i Warszawa w Katowicach* (*Katowice Man in Warsaw and Warsaw in Katowice*) "Opole", 1979

112. B. Kowalska *Wystawa obrazów* (*Exhibition of Paintings*), catalogue introduction, BWA "Gallery" "Arsenał", Poznań, 1979

113. K.T. Toeplitz *Wystawa obrazów* (*Exhibition of Paintings*), catalogue introduction, Regional Museum in Toruń, 1979; BWA "Gallery" in Olsztyn, 1979; TPS Gallery in Sopot, 1979

114. W. Wierzchowska *Wystawa obrazów* (*Exhibition of Paintings*), catalogue introduction, BWA "Gallery" in Wałbrzych, 1979; BWA "Gallery" in Koszalin, 1979

115. (r) *Wstrząsające malarstwo J. Dudy-Gracza* (*J. Duda-Gracz's Penetrating Painting*) "Express Poznański", 58, 1979

116. O. Błażewicz *Dużo dobrego malarstwa* (*A Good Deal of Good Painting*) "Głos Wielkopolski", 24–25 March, 1979

117. Jeden *Jak demaskować brzydotę* (*How You Debunk Ugliness*) "Głos Szczeciński", 64, 1979

118. J. Juszczyk *Z drugiej strony...* (*On the Other Hand...*) "Gazeta Zachodnia", 67, 1979

119. (il) *Wystawa malarstwa Dudy-Gracza* (*Exhibition of Duda-Gracz's Painting*) "Gazeta Olsztyńska" 76, 1979

120. H. Panas *Duda-Gracz* "Gazeta Olsztyńska", 83, 1979

121. O. Błażewicz *Piękno podejrzane Dudy-Gracza* (*Duda-Gracz's Suspect Beauty*) "Tydzień", 17, 1979

122. C.S. *Repräsentative Ausstellung* "Tageblatt", 80, 1979

123. J. Haak *Romans Dudy-Gracza* (*Duda-Gracz's Romance*) "Trybuna Wałbrzyska", 21, 1979

124. *Malarstwo bez maski* (*Undisguised Painting*) "Polska" 5, 1979 ("Poland" May, 1979)

125. I. Rajewska *Trzeba być sobie wiernym* (*One Has to Be True to Oneself*) "Panorama Północy", 19, 1979

126. (BETA) *Obrazów malowanie* (*Painting Pictures*) "Warmia i Mazury", 6, 1979

127. M. Sztokfisz *Duda-Gracz ty to masz dobrze* (*Aren't you lucky, Duda-Gracz?*) "Sztandar Młodych", 153, 1979

128. W. Skrodzki *Najciekawsza wystawa roku?* (*The Most Interesting Show of the Year?*) "Więź", 5, 1979

129. Laik *Świat Dudy-Gracza* (*Duda-Gracz's World*) "Dziennik Bałtycki", 168, 1979

130. Z. Florczak *Niepełny bilans naszej sztuki* (*Incomplete Balance of Our Art*), "Stolica", 29, 1979

131. N. Cieślińska *Brawo Duda, graj tak dalej* (*Bravo, Duda, Keep up the Tune*) "Sztuka", 1, 1979

132. (sok) *Malarstwo Jerzego Dudy-Gracza* (*Jerzy Duda-Gracz's Painting*) "Kurier Lubelski", 202, 1979

133. IJK *Hamlet polny i inni* (*Hamlet of the Fields and Others*) "Kamena", 21, 1979

134. M. Grudniewska *Iwona z girlandy* (*Iwona of the Garland*) "Bałtyk", 12, 1979

135. (KP) *Plon twórczych poszukiwań* (*The Crop of Creative Search*) "Wieczór", 253, 1979

136. M. Podolska *Naturą jest człowiek* (*Man Is Nature*) "Trybuna Robotnicza", 16–18 Nov, 1979

137. E. Łubowicz *Duda-Gracz* "Wieczór Wrocławia", 278, 1979

138. A. Wiśniewski *Gabinet śmiechu Dudy-Gracza* (*Duda-Gracz's Chamber of Laughter*) "Gazeta Robotnicza", 280, 1979

139. K.T. Toeplitz *Wystawa obrazów* (*Exhibition of Paintings*), catalogue introduction, BWA Gallery in Tarnów, 1980

140. W. Skrodzki *Wystawa obrazów* (*Exhibition of Paintings*), catalogue introduction, "Pryzmat" Gallery, Cracow, 1980

141. W. Wierzchowska *Wystawa obrazów* (*Exhibition of Paintings*), catalogue introduction, BWA Gallery in Jelenia Góra, 1980

142. Z. Jastrzębska *Jerzy Duda-Gracz* "Filipinka", 3, 1980

143. K. Młynarczyk *Apokalipsa dla maluczkich* (*Apocalypse for the Innocent*) "Poglądy", 2, 1980

144. H. Waniek *Duda-Gracz* "Twórczość", 12, 1979

145. *Wystawa obrazów Jerzego Dudy-Gracza* (*Exhibition of Paintings by Jerzy Duda-Gracz*) "Bydgoski Informator Kulturalny", 2, 1980

146. Z. Nowicka *Fascynujący świat Dudy-Gracza* (*Duda-Gracz's Fascinating World*) "Gazeta Pomorska", 40, 1980

147. A. Miecz *Wystawa obrazów, które szokują* (*Exhibition of Shocking Paintings*) "Dziennik Wieczorny", 42, 1980

148. M. Andrzejewski *Duda-Gracz obiecuje poprawę* (*Duda-Gracz Promises Improvemet*) "Dziennik Wieczorny", 49, 1980

149. (l) *„Brzydkie" obrazy* (*"Ugly" Paintings*) "Tarnowski Magazyn Informacyjny", 11, 1980

150. M. Ratajczak *Mięso* (*Flesh*) "Odra", 3, 1980

151. M. Bacciarelli *Nie udawajmy zdziwienia* (*Let's Not Pretend to be Surprised*) "Fakty", 11, 1980

152. E. Zaczyk *Tak to widzę* (*That's How I See It*) "Trybuna Robotnicza", 63, 1980

153. (j) *Duda-Gracz w Zakopanem* (*Duda-Gracz in Zakopane*) "Dziennik Polski", 23 April, 1980

154. S. Krzysztofowicz-Kozakowska *Przeciętność – obrzydliwa* (*Hideous Mediocrity*) "Życie Literackie", 14, 1980

155. Ł. Wyrzykowski *Być widzianym to więcej niż być* (*To Be Seen Is More than to Be*) "Dziennik Zachodni", 12–13 April, 1980

156. J. Madeyski *Jerzy Duda-Gracz* "Gazeta Południowa", 106, 1980

157. T. Nyczek *Duda-Gracz w "Pryzmacie"* (*Duda-Gracz at the "Pryzmat"*) "Echo Krakowa", 13 May, 1980

158. J.G. *Polaków portret własny ale inny* (*The Poles' Own Portrait but a Different One*) ''Gazeta Lubuska'', 123, 1980
159. M. Kitowska *Zdolny terminator czy polski Fellini?* (*Gifted Apprentice or a Polish Fellini?*) ''Ziemia Gorzowska'', 30 May, 1980
160. T. Nyczek *Osobny* (*The Separate One*) ''Sztuka'', 3, 1980
161. (ZOF) *Twórczość Dudy-Gracza w Jeleniej Górze* (*Duda-Gracz's Work in Jelenia Góra*) ''Słowo Polskie'', 147, 1980
162. I. Klisowska *Zdeformowane piękno* (*Beauty Deformed*) ''Informator Kulturalny woj. Jeleniogórskiego'', 6, 1980
163. A. Skoczylas *Dialog – sztuka publicystyczna* (*Dialogue – Journalistic Art*) ''Radar'', 8, 1980
164. M. Dunikowska *Wystawa, której się nie zapomni* (*Exhibition that We Shall Not Forget*) ''Wiadomości'', 36, 1980
165. M.A. Styks *Hamlet polny* (*Hamlet of the Fields*) ''Życie Literackie'', 34, 1980
166. (kk) *Kto kupi obrazy Dudy-Gracza* (*Who Will Buy Jerzy Duda-Gracz's Paintings*) ''Wieczór Wrocławia'', 36, 1981
167. T. Nyczek *Ciąg autoportretów* (*Series of Self-portraits*) ''ITD'', 16, 1981
168. J.P. *Jerzy Duda-Gracz* ''Radar'', 4, 1981
169. W. Skrodzki *Duda-Gracz* ''Messemagazin International'', 1981
170. P. Trzeciak *Zwierciadło moralisty* (*A Moralist's Mirror*) ''Panorama Polska'', 10, 1981
171. J. Jurczyk *Caprichos Dudy-Gracza* (*Duda-Gracz's Caprichos*) ''Głos Szczeciński'', 214, 1981
172. J. Braun *Jak Polak z Polakiem nie potrafi się dogadać* (*How Poles Cannot Come to Terms with One Another*) ''Echo Dnia'', 220, 1981
173. A. Zych *Manifestacja tego, jaki człowiek jest naprawdę* (*Manifestation of what Man Really Is*) ''Słowo Ludu'', 1162, 1981
174. T. Nyczek *Fotografie z karuzeli* (*Photographs from a Merry-go-round*) ''Pismo'', 5/6, 1981
175. L. Lameński *Malarstwo Jerzego Dudy-Gracza* (*Jerzy Duda-Gracz's Painting*) ''Akcent'', 2, 1982
176. K.T. Toeplitz *Między rozpaczą a drwiną* (*Between Despair and Derision*) ''Tu i Teraz'', 10, 11, 12, 1982
177. T. Kucharski *Co jest w środku Dudy-Gracza* (*What's Inside Duda-Gracz*) ''Tu i Teraz'', 30, 1982
178. V.D. Valitas *Obrazy polskie* (*Polish Paintings*), catalogue introduction, BWA Gallery in Łódź, 1983
179. K. Targosz *Czy jesteśmy tacy brzydcy?* (*Are We that Ugly?*) ''Panorama'', 11, 1983
180. B. Brózda *Czy Duda-Gracz lubi budowlanych?* (*Does Duda-Gracz Like Builders?*) ''Konstrukcje'', 13, 1983
181. T. Szyma *Jasnogórskie inspiracje* (*Inspirations from Jasna Góra*) ''Tygodnik Powszechny'', 14/15, 1983
182. M.A. Styks *Poświąteczne* (*The Feast Is Over*) ''Życie Literackie'', 15, 1983
183. I. Rajewska *Malarz polityczny?* (*Political Painter?*) ''Polityka'', 16, 1983
184. (dar) *Stąd świat widać lepiej, a człowieka bliżej* (*From Here One Sees the World Better and Man Closer*) ''Za i Przeciw'', 1983
185. B. Brózda *Pomijam cacane buziaczki brojlerów* (*I Walk Past Chicks' Lovely Phizs*) ''Walka Młodych'', 22, 1983
186. B. Kowalska *Polski sukces w Wenecji* (*Polish Success in Venice''*) ''Życie Literackie'', 22, 1984
187. J. Jerzewski *Wenecja po sarmacku* (*Venice Sarmatian Style*) ''Przekrój'', 2042, 1984
188. A. Baranowska *Sztuka i sztuki* (*Art and Arts*) ''Tu i Teraz'', 30, 1984
189. J. Duda-Gracz *O sobie* (*On Myself*) ''Projekt'', 3, 1984
190. T. Kucharski *Sukcesy cokolwiek pokraczne* (*Somewhat Hideous Success*) ''Tu i Teraz'', 46, 1984
191. M.A. Styks *Przegląd prasy* (*Press Review*) ''Życie Literackie'', 48, 1984
192. A. Fogtt *XLI Biennale Sztuki w Wenecji* (*41st Biennale of Art in Venice*) ''Sztuka'', 3, 1984

193. P. Rizzi, A. Scala "Il Gazzettino", 14 June, 1984
194. D. Micecchi "L'Unita", 10 June, 1984
195. D. Guzzi "L'Umanita", 15 June, 1984
196. W.K. *41 Biennale* (*41 Biennale*) "Dziennik Polski" (London), 1984
197. J. Karkoszka *Można Dudy-Gracza nie lubić...* (*One Doesn't Have to Like Duda-Gracz...*) "Trybuna Robotnicza", 11 Jan, 1985
198. R. Kosiński *W teatrze i u Dudy-Gracza* (*At the Theatre and at Duda-Gracz's*) "Trybuna Ludu", 13 Jan, 1985
199. T.L. *Galeria 40-lecia 'P' J. Duda-Gracz* (*Gallery of 'P''s 40 Years. J. Duda-Gracz*) "Przekrój", 2068, 1985
200. B. Lubosz *Archipelag Dudy-Gracza* (*Duda-Gracz's Archipelago*) "Panorama", 3, 1985
201. B. Brózda, *Malarska narracja czy obrzydzanie świata?* (*A Painter's Narration or Uglifying the World?*) "Odrodzenie", 6, 1985
202. R. Barnet *Cenię sobie porozumienie z drugim człowiekiem* (*I Appreciate Communication with Another Person*) "Express Wieczorny", 26, 1985
203. L. Michalski *Samowyobcowanie?* (*Self-alienation?*) "Tak i Nie", 4, 1985
204. A. Baranowska *Sztuka jako chleb powszedni* (*Art as the Daily Bread*) "Kobieta i Życie", 3, 1985
205. M. Gajewski *"Zachęta" żyje Dudą-Graczem* (*"Zachęta" Gallery Seething with Duda-Gracz*) "Sztandar Młodych", 29, 1985
206. B. Lubosz *Podróż do kresu obnażania* (*A Journey to the Limits of Denudation*) "Opole", 2, 1985
207. M. Gajewski *Dudy-Gracza portret Polaków* (*Duda-Gracz's Portrait of Poles*) "Sztandar Młodych", 38, 1985
208. T. Kucharski *Publicysta łamie... pędzel* (*A Journalist Breaks his Brush*) "Tu i Teraz", 8, 1985
209. A. Matynia *Duda-Gracz* "Tu i Teraz", 8, 1985
210. E. Andryszczak *Gdy rozum śpi...* (*When Reason Is Asleep...*) "Trybuna Ludu", 47, 1985
211. J. Paszkiewicz *Głos poza chórem* (*A Voice off the Choir*) "Radar", 9, 1985
212. W. Filler *Mistrz Duda-Gracz* (*Master Duda-Gracz*) "Gazeta Krakowska", 45, 1985
213. R.M. Groński *Pogoda Burzy* (*Stormy Weather*) "Polityka", 8, 1985
214. M. Prosna *Duda-Gracz w "Zachęcie"* (*Duda-Gracz at the "Zachęta"*) "Argumenty", 11, 1985
215. H. Sadowska *Kłopot z Dudą-Graczem* (*The Trouble with Duda-Gracz*) "Perspektywy", 10, 1985
216. H. Szczawińska *Malarstwo J. Dudy-Gracza* (*J. Duda-Gracz's Painting*) "Słowo Powszechne", 53, 1985
217. J. Duda-Gracz *Dlaczego maluję, dlaczego wystawiam* (*Why I Paint, Why I Exhibit*) "Polityka", 9, 1985
218. IJK *Ora et Colabora* "Kamena", 6, 1985
219. L. Kydryński *Kurier Warszawski* (*Warsaw Gazette*) "Przekrój", 2077, 1985
220. M. Obrembalska *Jerzy Duda-Gracz* "Barwy", 4, 1985
221. A.P. *Pasja według Dudy-Gracza* (*The Passion According to Duda-Gracz*) "Tygodnik Demokratyczny", 9, 1985
222. Kajot *Jerzy Duda-Gracz* "Szpilki", 12, 1985
223. Z. Jastrzębska *W Zachęcie wystawa obrazów...* (*Exhibition of Paintings at the Zachęta...*) "Filipinka", 6, 1985
224. A. Wilniewczyc *Módl się i współpracuj* (*Pray and Collaborate*) "Echo Dnia", 72, 1985
225. K.T. Toeplitz *Jerzy Duda-Gracz* "Arkady", Warsaw 1985
226. J. Bremer *Die Wohnung als Museum* "Frankfurter Allgemeine", 4 March, 1985
227. E. Heine *Kronika* (*Chronicle*) "Sztuka", 2/3, 1985
228. J. Szczupał *Jarmark* (*Fair*) "Trybuna Opolska", 115, 1985
229. A. Matynia *Dwa nurty* (*Two Trends*) "Tu i Teraz", 24 April, 1985

230. J. Madeyski *Duda-Gracz* "Życie Literackie", 15, 1985
231. *Jerzy Duda-Gracz houdt van ons land* "De Zwijndrechtse Kombinatie", 22 May, 1985
232. J. Jaremowicz *Jerzy Duda-Gracz* "Literatura", 6, 1985
233. P. Sanocki *Apocalypsis według Urbana* (*The Revelation According to Urban*) "Kultura Niezależ-na", 7, 1985
234. J. Jurczyk *Obrazy nie do sprzedania* (*Paintings Not for Sale*) "Morze i Ziemia", 24–30 July, 1985
235. J. Jurczyk *Formuła i Konkret* (*Formula and Hard Facts*) "Kultura", 11, 1985
236. M. Barański *Kocham Święty Spokój* (*I Love Being Let Alone*) "Warmia i Mazury", 15, 1985
237. B. Trześniewska *A Second Breughel? Our No. 1* "Poland", 1985
238. (mars) *Pierwsza na Śląsku* (*The First in Silesia*) "Dziennik Zachodni", 18 Dec, 1985
239. J. Karkoszka *Galeria autorska J. Dudy-Gracza* (*J. Duda-Gracz's Gallery D'Auteur*) "Trybuna Robotnicza", 18 Dec, 1985
240. M. Turski *Urodzona szczęśliwie w przepisowym czasie* (*Happy and Timely Delivery*) "Polityka", 1, 1986
241. S. Kobyliński *Objawienie Dudy-Gracza* (*The Revelation of Duda-Gracz*) "Tygodnik Kulturalny", 1, 1986
242. M. Kaniewski *Wernyhora z kabaretu* (*Wernyhora of a Cabaret*) "Tak i Nie", 1, 1986
243. M. Biernacka *Warszawska wystawa Dudy-Gracza* (*Duda-Gracz's Warsaw Exhibition*) "Więź", 6, 1985
244. A. Matynia *Droga* (*The Road*) "Projekt", 6, 1985
245. R. Kostorz *Prosta ludzka złość* (*Ordinary Human Anger*) "Tak i Nie", 5, 1986
246. M. Turski *Drugie zarzynanie koguta* (*The Second Slaughter of a Cock*) "Polityka", 4, 1986
247. T. Sernik *Świat w krzywym zwierciadle* (*The World in a Distorting Mirror*) "Dziennik Zachodni", 27, 1986
248. T. Gierzyńska *Z Düsseldorfu* (*From Düsseldorf*) "Sztuka", 6, 1986
249. D. Lubosz *Obrazy i Sława* (*Paintings and Fame*) "Opole", 2, 1986
250. T. Mullaly *Polish symbolist* "Daily Telegraph", 40, 1986
251. H. Blacker *Jerzy Duda-Gracz* "Visual Arts", 6 Feb, 1986
252. H. de Berchgrave *Jerzy Duda-Gracz* "Arts Review", 31 Jan, 1986
253. J. Sawtell *Integration of art and society transcends the past* "Morning Star", 24 Jan, 1986
254. H. de Berchgrave *The Manifesto of Jerzy Duda-Gracz* "Art Art" 3, 1986
255. R. Gołębiowska *Holenderskie sny J. Dudy-Gracza* (*J. Duda-Gracz Dutch Dreams*) "Dziennik Ludowy", 38, 1986
256. A. Matynia *Znani o znanych* (*The Familiar about the Familiar*) "Tak i Nie", 7, 1986
257. M. Skocza *Artyści potrafią nas rozgrzać* (*Artists Can Heat Us up*) "Dziennik Zachodni", 50, 1986
258. (bk) *Portrety Jerzego Dudy-Gracza* (*Portraits by Jerzy Duda-Gracz*) "Słowo Ludu", 58, 1986
259. (pik) *Portrety J. Dudy-Gracza w radomskim BWA* (*Portraits of Jerzy Duda-Gracz at the BWA Gallery in Radom*) "Życie Radomskie", 48, 1986
260. M. Szyjko *Portrety Dudy-Gracza* (*Portraits of Duda-Gracz*) "Tygodnik Radomski", 11, 1986
261. (JR) *Jerzy Duda-Gracz* "Rzeczpospolita", 66, 1986
262. H. Przedborska *Brawo Duda – graj tak dalej* (*Bravo Duda, Keep up the Tune*) "Dziennik Ludowy", 64, 1986
263. R. Gołębiowska *Duda-Gracz – gra inaczej* (*Duda-Gracz Has Changed the Tune*) "Tygodnik Kulturalny", 11, 1986
264. A. Popiel *Złudzenie holenderskie* (*Dutch Illusion*) "Tygodnik Demokratyczny", 8, 1986
265. W. Kiwilszo *Polska w Holandii* (*Poland in Holland*) "Stolica", 13, 1986
266. J. Jaremowicz *Duda-Gracz* "Nowe Książki", 3, 1986

267. A. Kaliszewski *Polaków portret ironiczny* (*The Poles' Ironical Portrait*) "Dziennik Polski", 83, 1986

268. *Jerzy Duda-Gracz* "Tekenen Schilderen", 4, 1986

269. (hld) *Duda-Gracz przy ulicy Długiej* (*Duda-Gracz in Długa Street*) "Głos Wybrzeża", 62, 1986

270. A. Pawlak *Piękne złudzenia Dudy-Gracza* (*Duda-Gracz's Beautiful Illusions*) "Dziennik Bałtycki", 63, 1986

271. E. Tosza *Kompleks polski Jerzego Dudy-Gracza* (*Jerzy Duda-Gracz's Polish Complex*) "Gazeta Krakowska", 80, 1986

272. A. Matynia *Droga z "Krzyżem polskim"* (*The Road with the "Polish Cross"*) "Tak i Nie", 1, 1986

273. J. Kamiński *Tropem wielbłąda* (*Trailing a Camel*) "Biuletyn Informacyjny", 4, 1986

274. *Duda-Gracz* "Sztuka", 1, 1986

275. J. Kossakowski *Nowość – galerie autorskie* (*Novelty: Galleries d'Auteur*) "Słowo Powszechne", 78, 1986

276. *Plastyka* (*Visual Arts*) "Życie Literackie", 21, 1986

277. (W. Jarz.) *Malarstwo Dudy-Gracza w Galerii Hasiora* (*Duda-Gracz's Painting at the Hasior Gallery*) "Dziennik Polski", 123, 1986

278. M. Wendrychowska *W stronę klasycznego piękna* (*Towards Classical Beauty*) "Wybrzeże", 21, 1986

279. R. Kosiński *Przed siebie, do wspomnień* (*Looking Forwards and Backwards*) "Trybuna Ludu", 126, 1986

280. W. Żukrowski *Moje śląskie gniazdo* (*My Silesian Nest*) "Dziennik Zachodni", 119, 1986

281. K. Brakoniecki *Obrazy jurajskie Jerzego Dudy-Gracza* (*Jerzy Duda-Gracz's Jurassic Paintings*) "Gazeta Olsztyńska", 132, 1986

282. K.B. *W BWA wielka wystawa Jerzego Dudy-Gracza* (*Jerzy Duda-Gracz's Big Show at the BWA Gallery*) "Gazeta Olsztyńska", 130, 1986

283. W. Kiwilszo *Autorska galeria Dudy-Gracza* (*Duda-Gracz's Gallery d'Auteur*) "Stolica", 25, 1986

284. S. Stopczyk *Jerzy Duda-Gracz* "Bildende Kunst", 6, 1986

285. M. Rosiak *Przeciw Matejce XX wieku* (*Against a 20th-century Matejko*) "Wprost", 7, 1986

286. O. Błażewicz *Duda-Gracz i pozostali...* (*Duda-Gracz and the Rest...*) "Głos Wielkopolski", 172, 1986

287. (nk) *Jerzy Duda-Gracz* "Polityka", 31, 1986

288. K. Gedroyć *Koniec żartów* (*The Joke's Over*) "Warmia i Mazury", 14, 1986

289. (kr) *Duda-Gracz w "Arsenale"* (*Duda-Gracz at the "Arsenal"*) "Kurier Podlaski", 156, 1986

290. J.A. Hermanowicz *Dlaczego nie lubię Dudy-Gracza?* (*Why I Don't Like Duda-Gracz?*) "Gazeta Współczesna", 195, 1986

291. (j.a.h.) *Jerzy Duda-Gracz w białostockim BWA* (*Jerzy Duda-Gracz at the BWA Gallery in Białystok*) "Gazeta Współczesna", 186, 1986

292. A. Zielińska *Dudy-Gracza powrót do przeszłości* (*Duda-Gracz's Return to the Past*) "Gazeta Współczesna", 189, 1986

293. H. Sandberg *Ein polnischer Goya* "Das Magazin", 8, 1986

294. A. Kochanowska *Kronika* (*Chronicle*) "Sztuka", 4, 1986

295. A. Koziara *Dziurawe Sztandary* (*Threadbare Banners*) "Kurier Podlaski", 12–14 Sept, 1986

296. R. Brzezińska *Dudy-Gracza refleksje malarskie* (*Duda-Gracz's Painted Reflections*) "Słowo Powszechne", 191, 1986

297. H. Richter *Vorschau auf 20. Art Cologne* "Weltkunst", 21, 1986

298. I. Rajewska *Kronika* (*Chronicle*) "Sztuka", 5, 1986

299. A. Matynia *Gombrowicz i Duda-Gracz* (*Gombrowicz and Duda-Gracz*) "Odrodzenie", 3, 1987

300. GoGa *Jerzy Duda-Gracz das Auge der 'Condition Polonaise'* "Vernissage", 1, 1987

301. M. Bijoch *Portret bez ram* (*Portrait without Frames*) "Reporter", 2, 1987

302. E. Karwowska *Maluję bo muszę* (*I Paint because I Have to*) "Głos Robotniczy", 36, 1987

303. R. Twardoch *Szczwany kocur patrzy na mnie i kpi* (*Crafty Cat Looks at Me and Mocks Me*) "Trybuna Robotnicza", 85, 1987

304. S. Skocza *W stronę Uniwersum* (*Towards the Universe*) "Dziennik Zachodni", 91, 1987

305. E. Pietroszka *W krzywym zwierciadle* (*In a Distorting Mirror*) "Panorama", 28, 1987

306. T.S. Jaroszewski *Rozważania nad portretem skandalicznym* (*On Scandalous Portraiture*) "Spotkania z zabytkami", 3 (31) Nov, 1987

307. J. Karkoszka *W gościnie u malarza* (*At the Painter's*) "Trybuna Robotnicza", 153, 1987

308. *Gesellschaftskritisches von Jerzy Duda-Gracz* "Diplomatic Correspondence", Vienna, 6–7, 1987

309. S. Stopczyk *Ekspresjonizm* (*Expressionism*) Krajowa Agencja Wydawnicza, Warsaw 1987

310. J. Kraszewski *250 obrazów Dudy-Gracza w Moskwie* (*250 Paintings by Duda-Gracz in Moscow*) "Trybuna Ludu", 192, 1987

311. M. Bierut *Polski dom otwarty w Szwecji* (*Polish Open House in Sweden*) "Gazeta Olsztyńska", 166, 1987

312. W. Wasilewski *Polskie malarstwo współczesne w moskiewskim Maneżu* (*Contemporary Polish Painting at the Moscow Manège*) "Trybuna Robotnicza", 169, 1987

313. W.S. Dębski *Prezentacja polskiego malarstwa* (*Presentation of Polish Painting*) "Trybuna Ludu", 169, 1987

314. *Plastyka* (*Visual Arts*) "Życie Literackie", 32, 1987

315. A.J. *Sich selbst begegnen* "Polen", 4 (352), 1987

316. (C.) *Wystawa J. Dudy-Gracza w Moskwie* (*J. Duda Gracz's Exhibition in Moscow*) "Rzeczpospolita", 192, 1987

317. (wow) *Zagraniczne wystawy łódzkiego BWA* (*Foreign Exhibitions of the BWA in Łódź*) "Głos Robotniczy", 183, 1987

318. (PAP) *Wystawa malarstwa J. Dudy-Gracza. Moskwa* (*Exhibition of J. Duda-Gracz's Painting. Moscow*) "Trybuna Robotnicza", 10 Aug, 1987

319. (c) *Wystawa malarstwa Jerzego Dudy-Gracza w Moskwie* (*Exhibition of Jerzy Duda-Gracz's Painting in Moscow*) "Dziennik Zachodni", 19 Aug, 1987

320. L. Grabarczyk *Bez znieczulenia* (*No Anaesthetics*) "Polsha", 8 (391), 1987

321. J. Kraszewski *Spotkanie obu stolic* (*Meeting of Two Capitals*) "Trybuna Ludu", 202, 1987

322. I. Pirogova *To Be One's Own Self* "Sovyetskaya Kultura", 104, 1987

323. *Moscow Private Views* "Moskovskaya Pravda", 194, 1987

324. *Plastyka* (*Visual Arts*) "Życie Literackie", 39, 1987

325. A. Matynia *Kryzys odbioru* (*Crisis of Reception*) "Odrodzenie", 36, 1987

326. C.M. Szczepaniak *Rodem z Familoków* (*Familok by Birth*) "Tygodnik Kulturalny", 39, 1987

327. (L.L.) *Polskie wystawy w Budapeszcie* (*Polish Exhibitions in Budapest*) "Trybuna Ludu", 209, 1987

328. J. Wędrowski *Nie tylko Jan III Sobieski... Not Only John III Sobieski...* "Gazeta Olsztyńska", 231, 1987

329. K.R. *Polscy plastycy za granicą* (*Polish Artists Abroad*) "Rzeczpospolita", 235, 1987

330. W. Krauze *Chełmska premiera* (*First Night in Chełm*) "Życie Warszawy", 247, 1987

331. M. Chrzanowski *Motyw polski* (*Polish Motif*) "Argumenty", 41, 1987

332. T. Rudomino *"Interart '87"* "Kultura", 44, 1987

333. (ben) *Milionowe zakupy na 'Interart '87'* (*One-million Pourchases at "Interart '87"*) "Kurier Polski", 231, 1987

334. P. Rejer *Sztuka liczenia pieniędzy* (*The Art of Counting Money*) "Sztandar Młodych", 235, 1987

335. (bk) *Efekty "Interartu"* (*Effects of "Interart"*) "Gazeta Poznańska", 280, 1987

336. K. Knapik *Duda-Gracz w Moscow* (*Duda-Gracz in Moscow*) "Szpilki", 45 (2389), 1987
337. J. Dombkowska *Duda-Gracz w Moskwie* (*Duda-Gracz in Moscow*) "Trybuna Ludu", 255, 1987
338. H. Richter *21 International Kunstmarkt* "Welt Kunst", 21, 1987
339. K. Koźniewski *Duda-Gracz* "Odrodzenie", 46, 1987
340. (-) "Sztuka Polska", 1 (40), 1987
341. J. Lutomski *Powstała Fundacja Kultury Polskiej* (*The Foundation of Polish Culture Has Been Launched*) "Rzeczpospolita", 297, 1987
342. W. Żukrowski *Prawdomówne zwierciadło* (*Truth-telling Mirror*) "Panorama", 52, 1987
343. W. Chmura *Bulion o zmierzchu we wsi Kamion* (*Broth at Dusk in the Village of Kamion*) "Nad Wartą", 40, 1987
344. A. Kochanowska *Kronika/Olsztyn* (*Chronicle/Olsztyn*) "Sztuka", 1, 1987
345. Compiled by T. Rudomino *O kiczu* (*On Kitsch*) "Sztuka", 2, 1987
346. B. Dyksińska-Tryc *Art Cologne* "Sztuka", 3, 1987
347. L. Pyetrova *Opinie o wystawie* (*Opinions of the Exhibition*) "Polsha", 1 (396) 1988
348. B. Pietkiewicz *Zabawnie tania sztuka* (*Amusingly Cheap Art*) "Polityka", 2 Jan, 1988
349. M. Kuc *"Interart '87"* "Tygodnik Kulturalny", 3 Jan, 1988
350. J. Miliszkiewicz *Przygody prywatnych mecenasów kultury* (*Adventures of Private Art Patrons*) "Słowo Powszechne", 12, 1988
351. *Personalia. Jerzy Duda-Gracz* (*Personal Data. Jerzy Duda-Gracz*) "Przegląd Tygodniowy", 4, 1988
352. A. Kobylińska *Kulturalna gala w MSZ* (*Cultural Gala at the Ministry of Foreign Affairs*) "Kurier Polski", 51, 1988
353. Ł. Wyrzykowski *Kultura śląska czy kultura na Śląsku* (*Silesian Culture or Culture in Silesia*) "Dziennik Zachodni", 53, 1988
354. J. Rey *Z perspektywy pępka* (*Seen from the Navel*) "Rzeczpospolita", 54, 1988
355. M.T. Kutiak *Czas na spokojną pracę* (*Time for Peaceful Work*) "Sztandar Młodych", 53, 1988
356. J.A. Rybczyński *Ballada o Kamionie* (*Ballad on Kamion*) "Głos Robotniczy", 34, 1988
357. E. Karwowska *Sztuka polska za granicą* (*Polish Art Abroad*) "Głos Robotniczy", 47, 1988
358. L. Wykrota *Reklama dźwignią kultury* (*Advertising Is the Pivot of Culture*) "Express Wieczorny", 17 March, 1988
359. M. Brzeźniak *Bizetowi to nie zaszkodzi* (*It Will Do Bizet No Harm*) "Trybuna Robotnicza", 29 March, 1988
360. J. Leszczyna *Nadal młody gniewny* (*An Angry Young Man After All*) "Trybuna Opolska", 29 March, 1988
361. S. Morawski *O sztuce zwanej religijną* (*On Art Called Religious*) "Więź", 10 April, 1988
362. *Sprzedajemy obrazy Jerzego Dudy-Gracza* (*Selling Jerzy Duda-Gracz's Pictures*) "Przekrój", 2236, 1988
363. V. Dittmar *Zeichen des Dämons* "Kultur Fürth", 26 April, 1988
364. (mars) *Zakochałam się w Dudzie-Graczu* (*I Fell in Love with Duda-Gracz*) "Dziennik Zachodni", 103, 1988
365. *Prowokacyjna "Carmen"* (*Provocative "Carmen"*) "Życie Warszawy", 12, 1988
366. M. Skocza *Z Dudą-Graczem na wabika* (*with Duda-Gracz as a Decoy*) "Dziennik Zachodni", 13, 1988
367. (R) *Triumf "Carmen"* (*The Triumph of "Carmen"*) "Wieczór", 13–15 May, 1988
368. M. Brzeźniak *Frywolna "Carmen"* (*Frivolous "Carmen"*) "Trybuna Robotnicza", 16 May, 1988
369. U. Orman *Kronikarz narodowych słabości* (*Chronicler of National Weaknesses*) "Gazeta Krakowska", 22 May, 1988

370. S. Rodziński *Malarstwo A. Mierzejewskiego* (*A. Mierzejewski's Painting*) "Tygodnik Powszechny", 5 June, 1988

371. K. Targosz *Jak przywrócić dawną świetność* (*How Can the Former Glamour Be Restored*) "Panorama", 24, 1988

372. E. Gretschel *4 mln złotych na konto Fundacji Kultury Polskiej* (*4 Million Zlotys to the Account of the Foundation of Polish Culture*) "Rzeczpospolita", 26 June, 1988

373. U. Orman *Trzy obrazy Dudy-Gracza poszły pod młotek* (*Three Paintings by Duda-Gracz Have Come under the Hammer*) "Gazeta Krakowska", 25–26 June, 1988

374. H. Dutkiewicz *Piąta "Carmen" na piątkę* (*Fifth "Carmen" Has Made the Grade*) "Tak i Nie", 26, 1988

375. M. Hałaś *Galeria przewrotnego mistrza* (*Gallery of a Wayward Master*) "Tak i Nie", 28, 1988

376. J. Wiśniewski *Grotesken im Zusammenleben* "Tagblatt für Österreich AZ", 16 June, 1988

377. *Zeitkritiker* "Neue Kronen Zeitung", 18 June, 1988

378. M. Buchsbaum *International Vielfalt der Kunst* "Wiener Zeitung", 16 June, 1988

379. *Jerzy Duda-Gracz in der BAWAG FONDATION* "Wirtschaft für Alle", June, 1988

380. L. Pyetrova *Finding the Essence* "Tvorchestvo", 5 (377), 1988

381. (at) *Malarstwo polskie we Lwowie* (*Polish Painting in Lvov*) "Trybuna Ludu", 28 Aug, 1988

382. I. Strzelewicz *Powroty, czyli obrazy jurajskie* (*Returns or Jurassic Paintings*) "TIM", 34, 1988

383. A. Tatarkiewicz *Dokąd?* (*Where to?*) "Polityka", 36, 1988

384. K.T. Toeplitz *Sztuka z wyjściem na ulicę* (*Art with an Exit to the Street*) "Polityka", 33, 1988

385. A.K. Olszewski *Dzieje sztuki polskiej 1890–1980 w zarysie* (*An Outline of the History of Polish Art 1890–1980*) Interpress, Warsaw 1988

386. B. Kowalska *Polska awangarda malarska 1945–1980 Szanse i mity* (*Avant-garde Polish Painting 1945–1980, Chances and Myths*) PWN (Scientific Publishers), Warsaw 1988

387. S.K. Stopczyk *Malarstwo polskie od realizmu do abstrakcjonizmu* (*Polish Painting from Realism to Abstraction*) KAW Publishers, Warsaw 1988

388. K. Koźniewski *Wściekli '88* (*The Mad Ones '88*) "Odrodzenie", 37, 1988

389. K. Karwat *Chodzę własnymi drogami* (*I Go My Own Way*) "Scena", 9, 1988

390. V. Balabanov *Jerzy Duda-Gracz's Theatre of Life* "Ogonyok", 48, 1988

391. *Jerzy Duda-Gracz* "BAUWAG", 1988

392. J. Duda-Gracz *Na portret* (*On Portrait*) "Sztuka", 5/6, 1988

393. M. Rostworowski *Jerzy Duda-Gracz – Portret Karola Estreichera* (*Jerzy Duda-Gracz. Portrait of Karol Estreicher*) "Sztuka", 5/6, 1988

394. J. Javošova *Optics of the Distorting Mirror* "Lietrárny Týždennik", 20 Jan, 1989

395. J. Miliszkiewicz *Pozujemy* (*Posing*) "Życie Warszawy", 14–15 Jan, 1989

396. W. Wierzchowska *Sąd nieocenzurowany* (*Uncensored Judgement*) "Film i Literatura" Publishers, Łódź 1989

397. I. Kamiński *Trudny romans z awangardą* (*Difficult Affair with Avant-garde*) Lubelskie Publishers, Lublin 1989

398. I. Strzelewicz-Ziemiańska *Żywa galeria* (*Lively Gallery*) "Panorama", 8 (1804), 1989

399. (ewka) *Wernisaż Jerzego Dudy-Gracza we Florencji* (*Opening of Jerzy Duda-Gracz's Exhibition in Florence*) "Trybuna Robotnicza", 23 Feb, 1989

400. W. Święcicki *Wioska artystyczna malowana obrazami* (*Art Village Lined with Paintings*) "Kurier Polski", 27 Feb, 1989

401. (zc) *Sztuka w Heweliuszu* (*Art at the Heweliusz*) "Express Wieczorny", 27 Feb, 1989

402. (-) *Simbolismo Duda-Gracz la Polonia e l'arte* "La Nazione" (Florence), 9 Feb, 1989

403. (-) *La Polonia vista da Gracz* "La Nazione" (Florence), 14 Feb, 1989

404. T. Paloscia *Pittura di denuncia sulla vita Polacca* "La Nazione", 4 March, 1989

405. B. Sośniarz *Najwięcej cenię pracowitość i upór* (*I Appreciate Diligence and Assiduity the Most*) "Wieczór", 40, 1989

406. K. Zboralska *Szarganie świętości* (*Desecration*) "Razem", 12 Feb, 1989

407. J. Miliszkiewicz *Wirus sztuki* (*The Virus of Art*) "Przegląd Tygodniowy", 10, 1989

408. (w) *Obrazy Dudy-Gracza we Włoszech* (*Duda-Gracz's Paintings in Italy*) "Express Wieczorny", 1 March, 1989

409. I. Gasz *Duda-Gracz za kartkami* (*Duda-Gracz behind Iron Bars*) "Nowiny Gliwickie", 27 March, 1989

410. M. Bacciarelli *Obrazek za cztery i pół miliona złotych* (*A Picture for Four and a Half Million Zlotys*) "Fakty", 13, 1989

411. I. Strzelewicz-Ziemiańska *Moja paranoja* (*My Paranoia*) "Sztandar Młodych, 19–21 May, 1989

412. R. Kosiński *O powietrzu, rocznicach, zabytkach i malarstwie* (*On the Air, Anniversaries, Monuments, and Painting*) "Trybuna Ludu", 9 June, 1989

413. (DAS) *Ojciec chrzestny – Jerzy Duda-Gracz* (*Jerzy Duda-Gracz the Godfather*) "Nad Wartą", 29, 1989

414. M. Koprowski *Dzwon na trwogę* (*The alarm bell Has been Sounded*) "Odgłosy", 31 (1635), 1989

415. M. Korotyńska *Hit sezonu* (*Hit of the Season*) "Dziennik Łódzki", 13 July, 1989

416. JAR *Duda-Gracz jak magnes* (*Duda-Gracz as a Magnet*) "Głos Robotniczy", 184, 1989

417. A. Matynia *Dzieciństwo Dudy-Gracza* (*Duda-Gracz's Childhood*) "Odrodzenie", 32, 1989

418. T. Rudomino *Artyści, krytycy i marszandzi* (*Artists, Critics and Dealers*) "Kultura", 35, 1989

419. A. Matynia *Odpowiedź panu Kringsowi* (*Answering Mr Krings*) "Kultura", 32, 1989

420. I. Strzelewicz-Ziemiańska *Odloty jesienne, droga pani* (*Autumn Departures, My Dear Lady*) "Sztandar Młodych", 13, 1989

421. S. Jordanowski *Vademecum malarstwa polskiego* (*Vademecum of Polish Painting*), Bicentennial Publishing Corp., New York

422. (s-ów) *Obrazy Dudy-Gracza na wystawie w Zamościu* (*Duda-Gracz's Paintings at the Exhibition in Zamość*) "Sztandar Ludu", 25, 1989

423. S. Mijas *Duda-Gracz w Miechowie* (*Duda-Gracz in Miechów*) "Słowo Ludu", 212, 1989

424. (mb) *Państwo Dzieduszyccy u Dudy-Gracza* (*The Dzieduszyccys' at Duda-Gracz's*) "Trybuna Robotnicza", 25 Oct, 1989

425. (jb) *Współczesny Medyceusz z Grosse Pointe* (*A Contemporary Medici of Grosse Pointe*) "Panorama Polska", 10 Oct, 1989

426. A. Matynia *Duda-Gracz i Gombrowicz* (*Duda-Gracz and Gombrowicz*) "Odrodzenie", 44, 1989

427. (maus) *Jerzy Duda-Gracz w Düsseldorf* (*Jerzy Duda-Gracz in Düsseldorf*) "Dziennik Zachodni", 10–12 Nov, 1989

428. *Das Schicksal als Groteske* "TOP", Winter 1989

429. *Plastyka* (*Visual Arts*) "Życie Literackie", 5 Nov, 1989

430. A. Osęka *Zgodnie z prawem, w imię porozumienia* (*In accordance with the Law, for the Sake of Understanding*) "Tygodnik Kulturalny", 26 Nov, 1989

431. (mb) *Wiesław Ochman gościem J. Dudy-Gracza* (*Wiesław Ochman at J. Duda-Gracz's*) "Trybuna Robotnicza", 7 Dec, 1989

432. J. Kossakowski *Galeria w Düsseldorfie Doroty Kabiesz* (*Dorota Kabiesz's Gallery in Düsseldorf*) "Słowo Powszechne", 31 Dec, 1989 – 1 Jan, 1990

433. (hg) *Malarstwo Dudy-Gracza* (*Duda-Gracz's Painting*) "Życie Pabianic", 4–10 Jan, 1990

434. (b) *Malarstwo Jerzego Dudy-Gracza* (*Jerzy Duda-Gracz's Painting*) "Życie Pabianic", 18–24 Jan, 1990

435. K. Lisiecki *Ciągle stoję po niewłaściwej stronie* (*I Am Always on the Wrong Side*) "Życie Pabianic", 3–4 Feb, 1990

JERZY DUDA-GRACZ wurde in 1941 geboren. 1968 absolvierte er in Katowice die Fakultät für Graphik der Akademie der Schönen Künste in Krakau. Er ist schöpferisch aktiv auf dem Gebiet der Malerei, Zeichnung und der breit aufgefaßten Gebrauchsgraphik. In das Bewußtsein des Publikums und der Kritiker drang er haftig Anfang der siebziger Jahre, als ein bereits voll geformter und seiner Botschaft bewußter Schöpfer, der alle Ziele und Richtungen der Wirkung kannte. Was fasziniert uns so in seinen Gemälden, die eingache und alltägliche Dinge darstellen? Warum werden die durchaus realistischen Bilder von Duda-Gracz mit Recht so begeistert aufgenommen in der Zeit, wo die klassische Figurenmalerei total aufgegeben wurde? Liegt der Grund dafür nich darin, daß uns der Künstler durch die Tiefe seiner Beobachtung, durch die Fähigkeit zur Synthese aller für das Bild und seinen Empfänger wesentlichen Elemente fasziniert? Duda-Gracz gibt nicht nur die Wirklichkeit wieder, sondern er verarbeitet sie vor allem und schafft die lapidaren Symbole und Synonyme der Ereignisse, die unsere bewegte Zeit bringt. Der Blick des Künstlers ist oft boshaft und ironisch und prangert kraftvoll unsere Mängel und Laster an; es fehlt ihm aber auch nicht an Lyrismus und Nachdenklichkeit, sowie an eigenartiger Wärme, die in allen, selbst den meist kritischen Gemälden zu finden ist. Der Künstler interessiert sich für den Menschen mit allen seinen Gegebenheiten, der die Ausgangsbasis für die Darstellung und Überlegung der allgemeineren Probleme, für die Reflexion über das Schicksal des Einzelnen und des Volkes wird.
Duda-Gracz zeichnet sich durch ungewöhnliche Kenntnis des Handwerks aus. Mit einer geradezu fotografischen Genauigkeit registriert er alle, selbst die scheinbar belanglosen Einzelheiten. Seine Bilder sind voller zahlreicher Details, köstlicher Stilleben sowie glanzvoll beobachteter und gemalter Landschaften, die in der gesamten Komposition eine wichtige Rolle spielen – zentralen Platz bleibt immer für den Menschen und seine gravierenden Probleme frei läßt. All das, durch das Prisma der künstlerischen Vision hindurchgegangen, bildet bestimmte Zusammenhänge und Komplexe der Formen und Inhalte und wird zu einer ''neuen Wirklichkeit'' mit dem bewußt mißgestalteten und bloßgestellten menschlichen Körper. Die Bilder von Duda-Gracz sind voller krummer und geschwollener Leiber, deren zu monströsen Ausmaßen vergrößerte einzelne Teile die Aufmerksamkeit des Zuschauers anziehen und bei ihm im ersten Augenblick das fröhliche und sorglose Gelächter hervorrufen. Doch bald zeigt es sich, daß neben den heiteren und pasticheartigen Elementen in diesen Bildern die bittere Reflexion und Nachdenklichkeit überwiegt.
Das ungewöhnlich sensible Auge des Künstlers, die Freiheit und Präzision im Handeln lassen auf der Leinwand die Szenen von geradezu surrealistischer Färbung und zugleich voller vitaler

Kraft entstehen, was in deren Schöpfer den Fortsetzer der interessantesten und wertvollsten Leistungen der niederländischen Kunst des 16. Jahrhunderts zu sehen erlaubt. Derjenigen Kunst, die die Aufmerksamkeit auf die Schönheit der heimischen Natur, vor allem aber auf den Menschen und sein Leben mit der Arbeit, der Erholung, dem Spiel und Vergnügen lenkte. Es muß deswegen die leider treffende Bemerkung von Wojciech Skrodzki überraschen, daß ''die Malerei von Jerzy Duda-Gracz im professionellen Künstlermilieu meistens sehr ungern geduldet wird''... (''Więź'' 1979, Heft 5). Zum Glück schafft dieser Künstler nicht für die Kritiker und Fachkollegen, sondern – wie es sich dem rassigen ''Renaissanceschöpfer'' ziemt – hauptsächlich für den Empfänger, der auf sein Schaffen stark emotionell reagiert.

Lechosław Lameński
Deutsch von Krzysztof Żak

Table of contents

Photographs by Małgorzata Apathy, Krzysztof Henclewski
1–43, 56–58; Zdzisław Sowiński 44–53, 55; Zbigniw Kamy-
kowski 59–64; Zbigniew Włodarski 54

Technical Editor:
Zbigniew Weiss

Proofreader:
Ewa Błażkow

Editor:
Maja Płażewska

CIP — Biblioteka Narodowa

Duda-Gracz Jerzy
Jerzy Duda-Gracz / [introd. Krzysztof Teodor
Toeplitz ; transl from Pol. Joanna Holzmann]. —
Warsaw : ,,Arkady'', 1992

The Publishing House Arkady, Warsaw 1992
First Edition. Symbol 1386/1/RS
Set by Comptext, Warsaw
Printed and bound in Slovenia